SRA Art Connections

Artist Profiles

Level 3

**SRA
McGraw-Hill**

Columbus, Ohio

*A Division of The **McGraw·Hill** Companies*

Cover: Joseph Jean-Gilles. (Haitian). *Haitian Landscape.* 1976. Museum of the Americas, Washington, DC.

SRA/McGraw-Hill

A Division of The **McGraw·Hill** *Companies*

Copyright © 1998 SRA/McGraw-Hill.

Send all inquiries to:
SRA/McGraw-Hill
250 Old Wilson Bridge Road
Suite 310
Worthington, OH 43085

Printed in the United States of America.

ISBN 0-02-688341-4

1 2 3 4 5 6 7 8 9 POH 01 00 99 98 97

Table of Contents

Berenice Abbott (ber ə nēs´ ab´ ət)
(1898 – 1991)

Born in Ohio, Abbott traveled to Europe to study drawing and sculpture. By chance, she became the darkroom assistant for a photographer in France. This temporary job led to her life-long interest in photography. By 1926, she had opened her own studio in Paris. While taking pictures of famous artists and writers, Abbott met an unknown photographer named Eugène Atget. She recognized his great talent and, after his death, saved his work from being destroyed. Through her efforts, Atget's photographs have been seen and admired worldwide.

Abbott moved back to the United States in 1929. Settling in New York City, she spent several years taking black-and-white photographs of the city. Her pictures recorded dramatic changes during that time. They were later published in a book titled *New York in the Thirties*. Abbott also photographed the countryside along U.S. Route 1, from Florida to Maine. Later she became fascinated with scientific photography. She found ways to show the motion of objects in photographs. To examine subjects close-up, Abbott took pictures through microscopes. Her photographs were so detailed that they were used in textbooks. Her work was also displayed in museums.

ABOUT ART HISTORY

Abbott contributed to photography with her own pictures of people, the changing landscape, and objects in motion. She also added to the world's art collection by preserving the work of Eugène Atget.

ABOUT THE ARTWORK

Abbott's work ranges from portraits of well-known people, to striking photographs of New York City and quiet scenes along Route 1, to remarkable

Yousuf Karsh/Woodfin Camp & Associates

pictures that show objects moving through space.

ABOUT THE MEDIA

Abbott was a photographer. She used cameras and microscopes.

ABOUT THE TECHNIQUE

Abbott felt that her training in sculpture helped her use light in her photographs. She said, "Photography is not only drawing with light. . . . It is modeling or sculpturing with light. . . ."

1

Charles Burchfield (chärlz bûrch´fēld)
(1893 – 1967)

About the Artist

After high school, Charles Burchfield attended the Cleveland School of Art. He supported himself by working in industry. He served in the armed forces during World War I. After the war, he worked as a wallpaper designer. Burchfield began painting in 1915 and specialized in painting American small-town scenes and country life. In 1929, he was able to support himself as a full-time painter. After 1943, he concentrated on painting landscapes in watercolor. He was married and had five children.

Tom Hollyman

ABOUT ART HISTORY

Burchfield was one of the first American scene painters. His art style shifted from fantasy to realism and back to fantasy. In his early paintings, for example, buildings have faces. Later, he painted similar scenes but in a very realistic style. Still later, fantasy found its way back into his landscapes. He used symbols to represent emotions. A hooked spiral might mean fear. Burchfield based some of his last paintings on his earliest ones. He called these "reconstructions."

ABOUT THE ARTWORK

Many of Burchfield's landscapes are based on two cities where he lived: Salem, Ohio, and Buffalo, New York. Burchfield stressed the loneliness and dreariness he saw there. He also focused on the beauty in nature. He often had one lone tree as the center of a painting. Some of Burchfield's trees were realistic, and some were imaginary. His paintings show his deep interest in the weather and changing seasons.

ABOUT THE MEDIA

Burchfield worked in watercolors and sometimes in pencil.

ABOUT THE TECHNIQUE

Burchfield was interested in sounds and tried to symbolize them in his paintings. For example, he used wavy lines to show the hammering sound of a woodpecker. Small spots of black paint in some of his pictures represented musical notes. Burchfield used ideas from his earlier work as a wallpaper designer. He might fit sheets of paper together to make large paintings. This way, he could take out parts he didn't like and add new parts.

About the Artist

Mrs. Andy G. Byler lived in Atlantic, Pennsylvania. She was an Amish woman. The Amish are a religious group that does not believe in decoration. They settled in the rich farmland of Pennsylvania during the colonial period. By rejecting modern conveniences, such as electricity, cars, and telephones, the Amish have managed to keep themselves separate from people who do not share their religious beliefs.

ABOUT ART HISTORY

The Amish learned how to make quilts after coming to the United States. Although the Amish community discourages making art, they like beautiful things if those things have practical uses. They have been making quilts since the 1830s. Most of the quilts are used on Amish beds for warmth. Sometimes the Amish give each other quilts as gifts for special occasions like weddings. They sell some quilts to the public.

Mrs. Andy G. Byler. (American). Double Wedding Ring Quilt. *c. 1920–1935. From the permanent collection of the Museum of American Folk Art, New York, New York. Gift of Mrs. Andy G. Byler.*

ABOUT THE MEDIA

Quilts are made of cotton, wool, linen, or synthetic fabrics. There are three layers of material in a quilt: the top cloth, the batting in the middle, and the bottom cloth. The three layers are stitched together with thread and a needle. Sometimes hoops or frames are used to hold the quilt in place while someone is working on it.

ABOUT THE ARTWORK

This quilt was made in the "Double Wedding Ring" design. The pattern was invented in the nineteenth or early twentieth century and is extremely popular but very difficult to make. The "Double Wedding Ring" design shows interlocking rings. Sometimes there are only two rings, but usually the quilt is covered with many interlocking rings. There are more than 38 known "Double Wedding Ring" styles of quilts. The Amish used bright fabrics set against dark backgrounds. They used only solid-colored fabrics in their quilts.

ABOUT THE TECHNIQUE

The Amish make a type of quilt known as a pieced quilt. First, they carefully plan the quilt pattern and draw it on paper. They cut out the pattern pieces and then trace them onto pieces of cloth with chalk or pencil. They cut out the pieces of cloth and sew them together. This makes the top cloth. Batting is sandwiched between the backing cloth and the top cloth. Then all the layers are stitched together. The Amish always sew their quilts by hand. Because they do not believe in using electricity, they do not use sewing machines.

Alexander Calder (a leg zan´ dər kôl´ dər)
(1898 – 1976)

About the Artist

Calder's mother was a painter, and both his father and grandfather were sculptors. Calder liked to make gadgets. He trained to be an engineer. Later, he attended art school and worked as a commercial artist. In 1926, he moved to Paris and began to experiment with making tiny circuses out of wood, cork, and wire. In 1931, he used his training as an engineer to create motor-driven sculptures. A year later, he invented *mobiles,* sculptures that move in the wind.

Calder traveled to France, South America, and Asia with his wife and two daughters. He created works of art wherever he went. His work became very popular. It has appeared in many public buildings, including the UNESCO headquarters in Paris and the Lincoln Center for the Performing Arts in New York City.

He never named his work until it was placed in its setting. His last mobile was hung in the East Wing of the National Gallery of Art in Washington, DC after he died and remains untitled.

ABOUT ART HISTORY
Calder was one of the first artists to create mobiles. He also produced what he called *stabiles.* These sculptures look like mobiles, but they do not move. Calder sometimes combined mobiles with stabiles. Much of Calder's work is abstract. For example, his sculpture *Hanging Spider* suggests a spider but does not have eight legs. Calder's style was influenced by his friendship with the surreal painters Joan Miró and Piet Mondrian.

ABOUT THE ARTWORK
Calder meant for his sculptures to suggest movements and shapes from nature, such as

Dominique Berretty/Black Star

clouds, leaves, or waves. Some of his works are very large. For example, a wire sculpture of a woman, called *Spring,* is seven feet high.

ABOUT THE MEDIA
Calder created his mobiles from wire and metal, balancing them carefully so they moved in the slightest breeze. He also made drawings, paintings, prints, and stage sets.

ABOUT THE TECHNIQUE
Calder usually began a large sculpture by first creating a small-scale model. Then he directed the making of the final sculpture.

Emily Carr (em´ə lē kär)
(1871–1945)

About the Artist

Carr was born in British Columbia, Canada. She liked to paint and draw even as a child, but her family did not encourage her. Her parents died when she was a teenager. Carr had many emotional and physical problems. A born rebel, she always thought of herself as different from other people. While struggling to establish herself as an artist, she taught art classes, grew fruit, raised hens and rabbits, and made pottery and rugs to support herself. She also spent long periods in hospitals. Between hospitalizations, Carr visited Native American reservations. She admired the people and their art and began to paint them.

The head of an Ottawa art museum saw her work and recognized her skills. Carr later met the Group of Seven, young Canadian artists who were experimenting with painting. At last she belonged to a community, and she began to paint full time. Nevertheless, Carr was in her late sixties before she made a living from her art. When heart attacks slowed her down, she turned to writing. Her books, including her autobiography *Growing Pains,* became even more popular than her paintings.

ABOUT ART HISTORY
Carr developed her own painting style. She was influenced by two years she spent in France, 1910 to 1912. After this trip, she began to paint in an impressionist style. She used forceful brush strokes and strong colors, and her art showed energy.

ABOUT THE ARTWORK
Carr focused on two subjects—Native Americans and the rain forests of British Columbia. Her paintings document a Native American way of life that has since disappeared.

BC Archives & Records Service, catalog #HP 44882

ABOUT THE MEDIA
Carr worked in watercolors and oils.

ABOUT THE TECHNIQUE
To save money, Carr sometimes used cheap paper and white house paint thinned with gasoline. She loved to paint outdoors where the view was "fresh." Carr often painted the same scene in the morning, after lunch, and in the early evening to try out different kinds of light. Some critics consider these quick paintings her best work.

Allen E. Cole (al´ ən kōl)
(1893 – 1970)

About the Artist

American photographer Allen E. Cole is known for his pictures of the Great Depression of the 1930s. Cole did not plan to be a photographer. After high school, he graduated from college and worked as a railroad porter, a real estate developer, and a waiter. Then he turned to photography. He opened a studio and started his career before the depression began. His skills allowed him to make a lasting contribution to people's understanding of daily life during the Great Depression.

ABOUT ART HISTORY
Cole's pictures of Cleveland during the 1930s are sometimes compared to those of James Van der Zee, who photographed Harlem during the 1960s. Cole's photographs, like Van der Zee's, invite viewers to better understand a group of people and the stressful time in which they lived.

ABOUT THE ARTWORK
Cole's work shows the richness and variety of life for African Americans in Cleveland during the Great Depression. He photographed groups and individuals, creating 30,000 negatives and 6,000 prints during his lifetime. His pictures offer glimpses of African American social, cultural, business, and religious groups who struggled and often succeeded during the depression.

The Western Reserve Historical Society, Cleveland, Ohio

ABOUT THE MEDIA
Cole produced black-and-white photographs.

ABOUT THE TECHNIQUE
Cole did not snap informal pictures. Instead, he carefully posed people to get the best visual effect. He included details in each photograph to help viewers understand the lives of the people. For example, a photograph he took in 1935 shows young newsboys gathered around a shiny bicycle. The photograph suggests that a bicycle was the center of these boys' lives because it helped them make a living. However, it is clear that their bikes were rarely as shiny and new as the one in the picture.

About the Artist

John Singleton Copley was born in Boston one year after his parents had come from Ireland. His father died, and his mother supported them by running a tobacco shop. When Copley was eleven, his mother married Peter Pelham who was a printmaker, a painter, and a teacher. Pelham quickly saw young Copley's talent and gave him his first art lessons. He also learned from studying prints of paintings by Michelangelo, Raphael, and Rubens.

In 1774, he was encouraged to come to Europe to study. He left his family in Boston and toured Europe. His father-in-law was one of the importers of that famous shipment of tea that was dumped in Boston Harbor. Because of that incident, his father-in-law left the Colonies in anger, taking Copley's wife and children with him to London.

Copley enjoyed brief success in London. At first his art was appreciated and earned high prices. He was not used to painting portraits in only five one-hour sessions, as was the custom in London. He soon fell out of fashion. His life ended on a sad note. He was in debt and missed America.

ABOUT ART HISTORY

Copley was one of the finest American artists of colonial times. In his early paintings in Boston, Copley wanted to show people as they were. His paintings were said to be "more real than real." After he moved to England, his work was influenced by English and other European painters. It lost some of its energy and realism.

ABOUT THE ARTWORK

Among Copley's early portraits were those of such American patriots as Paul Revere and John Hancock. He also painted English patriots who opposed America's independence. After moving to England, Copley began painting dramatic historical events.

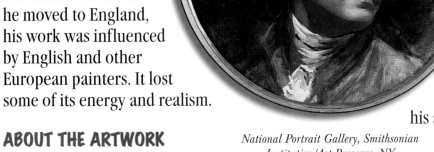

National Portrait Gallery, Smithsonian Institution/Art Resource, NY

ABOUT THE MEDIA

Copley worked primarily in oils.

ABOUT THE TECHNIQUE

Copley brought life to his early paintings by including objects used by his subjects in their daily lives. He was especially skillful at capturing his subjects' eyes. Through their eyes, he tried to show their characters. The people in his early portraits looked so real that John Adams, who became the second President of the United States, imagined he could talk to them and get answers!

7

Willis "Bing" Davis (wil´is bing dā´vəs)
(1937–   )

About the Artist

Davis was born in Dayton, Ohio. He was a student with many talents and gifts, including those for athletics and the arts. Because he excelled in sports, he was awarded a scholarship to DePauw University in Indiana. There, he earned a degree in art education. He continued to study and earned his master's degree from Miami University in Oxford, Ohio. Davis has pioneered such projects as the Dayton-based, now national, program "Artists in the Schools." Davis has also had more than fifty one-person art exhibits since 1959.

Courtesy of Bing Davis. Photo by Melvin Greer.

ABOUT ART HISTORY

Davis's style is a combination of African and African American styles. A fellowship to the country of Nigeria led him to explore the customs and the heritage of his ancestors. This understanding of where he comes from both spiritually and ethnically is incorporated into his artwork.

ABOUT THE ARTWORK

Davis's artwork pays tribute to his African culture. He transfers his ideas from one medium to the next. For example, he approaches much of his work in clay in the same way as he does collage. Davis is more concerned with the messages in his art than with preparing works just for exhibition.

ABOUT THE MEDIA

The works of Willis Davis are made from multiple mediums. He is a ceramist, photographer, jewelry maker, painter, and graphic artist. Drawing from an unlimited source of mediums allows Davis a freedom of expression. He also relies a great deal on found objects to get the message of his artwork across to the viewer.

ABOUT THE TECHNIQUE

Many of Davis's artistic works have come from an inquiry into his heritage. His art has been called "Visual Music." It is difficult to pinpoint a singular technique of Davis. His methods are a reflection of the diversity that he sees in the world. His ever-changing technique accommodates his ever-changing global perspective.

Edgar Degas (ed´ gär dā gä´)
(1834 – 1917)

About the Artist

Degas was born in Paris to a well-to-do family. He studied law for a short time before discovering his interest in painting. Degas studied briefly at the École des Beaux-Arts in Paris around 1855. He worked at an artist's studio and traveled widely to study art. His early work showed a concern with classical painting, in subject matter as well as composition. His themes always deal with people and city life, especially dancers at the theater. After 1909, Degas turned to sculpture due to failing eyesight. He left many wax models of dancers and horses that were cast into bronze after his death.

ABOUT ART HISTORY

Degas joined the Impressionist group and exhibited with them, even though he detested the name and never painted in a purely Impressionist style. He admired Italian Renaissance painters, such as Leonardo da Vinci. He also admired the French neoclassical painter Ingres, whose figures had the grace of Greek statues. In his own work, Degas combined Impressionism with the painting style of the Renaissance.

Francis G. Mayer/Corbis

ABOUT THE MEDIA

Degas created oil paintings, pastel drawings, ink drawings, and bronze sculptures. He also produced a great number of lithographs, engravings, and monotypes.

ABOUT THE TECHNIQUE

Many Impressionists painted outdoors and quickly. Degas chose to work in his studio, slowly. He planned his pictures and completed sketches before he painted. He sometimes took paintings back after they had been sold so he could "improve" them. He applied paint sketchily to make his work look unplanned.

Degas wanted his subjects to look as if they did not know they were being painted. He cut figures off at the edges of the canvas to make his pictures seem unposed. He also wanted viewers to feel as if they were part of the picture. For this reason, Degas included large, open spaces to allow viewers into his paintings.

ABOUT THE ARTWORK

Degas is famous for his portraits, especially of ballet dancers. Unlike other Impressionists, he enjoyed painting genre scenes of modern life. His painting of customers in a hat shop, for example, was unusual. At that time, artists did not usually paint such ordinary places.

André Derain (än drā´ də ran´)
(1880 – 1954)

About the Artist

This French artist studied engineering before deciding to become a painter. After attending an art school in Paris, he served three years in the military, painting in his free time. Derain's friend Matisse encouraged him to exhibit his paintings. Soon Derain was considered part of Matisse's fauvist movement, a group of painters who used brilliant, almost violent, colors in their art. Derain also began to sculpt, first in wood and then in stone. He liked to try different artistic styles and did not hesitate to return to traditional approaches. During Derain's lifetime, some people rejected his work when it no longer seemed to be on the cutting edge of modern art. His work is greatly admired today.

ABOUT ART HISTORY

Derain's artistic style was influenced by Gauguin, Cézanne, Matisse, Picasso, and his extensive readings in philosophy. He studied many painting styles, from primitive to Renaissance, and he experimented with different techniques. His painting *The Barges* is fauvist, while his *Collioure,* a seaside scene, is impressionistic. *The Window,* a view of a cross on a hill, is realistic. Derain did not admire originality; instead, he tried to use the best of the past in his work.

ABOUT THE ARTWORK

Derain painted still lifes, portraits, and some landscapes. He also painted scenes with religious references, such as *Calvary* in which dishes and a coffeepot on a table

French Cultural Services/Laurie Platt Winfrey/Woodfin Camp & Associates

represent the Last Supper. Derain was fascinated with ballet and theater. He designed costumes and sets for several productions. He also illustrated many books with his paintings and woodcuts.

ABOUT THE MEDIA

This artist expressed his ideas in oil paintings; wood, stone, and steel sculptures; drawings, lithographs, woodcuts, and etchings; and clay masks and figures.

ABOUT THE TECHNIQUE

Derain studied art styles extensively and made numerous sketches and drawings before choosing a way to portray a specific subject. His approach to art was thoughtful and analytical rather than emotional.

Albert Edward Edensaw

(al bərt´ ed wərd ē dən shä) *(c. 1812–1894)*

About the Artist

Albert Edward Edensaw was born around 1912 in a small village on the eastern shore of Graham Island. He was given the name Gwaigu-unlthin at his birth. He took the name Edensaw when he succeeded his uncle as Haida chief, and was named Albert Edward after the late king of England. Edensaw was a wealthy and powerful chief of the Haida Eagle clan and was often contacted to lead exploring parties around the island. Albert Edward Edensaw taught his nephew, Charles Edensaw, much about Haida art and mythology. Charles Edensaw became a well-known sculptor, metalworker, and painter.

ABOUT ART HISTORY

The Haida are Native Americans who live on the Queen Charlotte Islands off the coast of British Columbia. Supporting themselves by fishing and hunting, the Haida are well-known for their woodworking skills. From the red cedar of the surrounding rain forest, they have carved canoes, boxes, masks, and totem poles that record family histories. They also document their beliefs and traditional myths in wood.

ABOUT THE ARTWORK

Edensaw's headdress frontlet depicts a Haida story derived from the oral tradition of his clan. The carving represents a man who captured and killed a powerful sea monster, Gonakadeit. He wore the monster's skin, allowing him to swim deep in the ocean and capture many fish to feed his whole village. This headdress frontlet shows a man in a crouched position, wearing the sea monster's skin and holding a whale.

Albert Edward Edensaw. Kaigani Haida. Dancing Headdress Frontlet. *1860–1870. Maple and abalone shell. $6\frac{1}{4} \times 5\frac{7}{8} \times 2\frac{1}{4}$ inches. The Seattle Art Museum, Seattle, Washington. Gift of John H. Hauberg. Photo by Paul Macapia.*

ABOUT THE MEDIA

Edensaw carved the headdress from maple. It was painted and decorated with iridescent blue abalone shells.

ABOUT THE TECHNIQUE

Most Haida carvers created their own tools. Some carving tools had stone blades, while others had blades of shell or steel. Besides chisels, carvers used simple drills that they rotated between their palms. They gave their work a smooth finish by rubbing it with fine sandstone or sharkskin.

Philip Evergood (fil´ əp ev´ ər gûd)
(1901 – 1973)

About the Artist

Evergood was born in New York. His parents sent him to boarding schools in England and then to Cambridge University. He studied art briefly in Paris. He taught himself to be a painter against his parents' wishes. For several years, he traveled back and forth between Europe and the United States. He spent the 1930s, the years of the Great Depression, in America. He used his paintings to protest people's suffering. Evergood cared about human suffering and injustice, but he also had a temper. He could be demanding and hard to get along with. He married a ballet dancer who lived with him only on weekends. He had no children but loved his dogs. His life was a series of accidents and illnesses, ending in a fire in 1973. Evergood believed that his work would not be appreciated until after his death. He kept careful records of his life and art for those who might want to know about him.

ABOUT ART HISTORY
Evergood's paintings were brutally realistic during the 1930s. They became less harsh later in his life. Many art critics did not accept him, because he set his own rules. But he had great artistic talent. Evergood used his paintings to try to create a better world.

ABOUT THE ARTWORK
Evergood painted ordinary people, especially those who faced great odds. One example is his painting *My Forebears Were Pioneers.* In it, an old woman sits calmly amid the ruins of her home after a hurricane.

PACH/Corbis-Bettmann

ABOUT THE MEDIA
This artist began his career by painting murals for the Federal Art Project during the Great Depression. He worked mainly in oils.

ABOUT THE TECHNIQUE
Evergood painted in a fresh, simple style, almost like a child's. His work was sometimes thought of as "raw" and unfinished. He did not try to show depth. Thus, all objects appear to be beside each other. In his early paintings, he often used colors that clashed, such as reds and oranges. Later, he used more pleasing combinations.

Janet Fish (jan´ ət fish)
(1938 –   )

About the Artist

Fish earned two degrees in fine arts from Yale University but struggled to find work. For a while, she supported herself by painting bars of soap for a department store. Since then, her large, lively still lifes have become much admired. She has taught at art schools across the nation. She now spends half her time in New York City and half in Vermont.

Ann Chwatsky

ABOUT ART HISTORY
During the 1960s, Fish was part of a group of nontraditional painters. She is known as a realistic painter, but her work often has some abstract qualities. For example, she might exaggerate the shapes of bottles and repeat those shapes within a painting.

ABOUT THE ARTWORK
Fish's still lifes, landscapes, and portraits make everyday objects seem extraordinary. She might begin with a bottle of window cleaner or gummy candy. Then she uses them to create a fascinating combination of colors, contrasting surfaces, and light. She is especially interested in the effects of light. For example, she might show how it shines through a crystal bowl or on cut flowers.

ABOUT THE MEDIA
Fish's work includes both oil paintings and watercolors.

ABOUT THE TECHNIQUE
Fish carefully chooses and arranges the objects in her still lifes. She tries to feel her own connection to the objects and to understand how the objects relate to one another. She is concerned about color, texture, and balance in her paintings. To increase the impact of her work, she often paints objects three or four times larger than they really are. They usually fill the picture, crowding right up to the edge. Fish aims to paint still lifes that do not hold still.

Audrey Flack (ô´ drē flak)
(1931 –   )

About the Artist

Flack grew up in New York City and still lives there. She earned a fine arts degree from Yale. She also studied anatomy, the structure of the human body. This helped her make her paintings more realistic. Flack is married to a musician. Early in her career, she painted while raising two daughters. She also taught at Pratt Institute and New York University.

Audrey Flack. (American). Self-Portrait (the Memory). *1958. Oil on canvas. 50 × 34 inches. Art Museum Miami University, Oxford, Ohio.*

ABOUT ART HISTORY

Flack was a leader of the photo-realists in the 1970s. She was one of the first artists to base paintings on photographs. Her work also reflects strong influences of the feminist movement, which grew during the 1970s. Many of her still lifes are jammed and cropped like Old Master works.

ABOUT THE ARTWORK

Flack has painted large abstract images, smaller realistic still lifes, portraits, landscapes, and seascapes. She has also created photo-realistic paintings based on news stories. An example is *Kennedy Motorcade,* which focuses on the day President Kennedy was killed. Flack sometimes includes herself in her art. For instance, she placed a photo of herself in a painting of Marilyn Monroe. She means to show that certain issues, such as the role of women, are important to her. Since 1983, Flack has worked mainly at sculpting because she likes its solid feel. Many of her sculptures look like ancient Greek goddesses in modern settings.

ABOUT THE MEDIA

Flack works in oils, acrylics, watercolors, and bronze sculpture.

ABOUT THE TECHNIQUE

In her photo-realistic work, Flack painted from slides projected onto canvas. At one time, she used commercial slides and postcards. Later she worked from color slides she took herself. She uses an airbrush to apply paint.

Jane Freilicher (jān frī´ lik ər)
(1924 –)

About the Artist

Freilicher was born in New York City. She earned degrees from Brooklyn College, Columbia University, and the Hofmann School of Fine Arts. Since then, she has taught art at various colleges. When she began her career, Freilicher just wanted to see if she could paint. As she improved her skills, painting turned into a career. She had her first one-person show in 1952, at the age of 28. Since then, her work has been hung in many galleries and included in many collections. She has won a number of awards, including a National Endowment for the Arts Grant in 1976.

ABOUT ART HISTORY
Freilicher painted in a mostly realistic style until the 1980s. Then her work shifted somewhat toward abstract expressionism. She paints what she experiences rather than exactly what she sees. Freilicher might even be described as a regionalist. She paints landscapes in only one region—Long Island Sound.

ABOUT THE ARTWORK
Freilicher paints what she sees through her studio window. Her window overlooks the sound and low-lying islands. She usually includes the window frame and a vase of flowers on a table in the foreground. Thus, she combines landscape with still life. The pictures vary with the seasons, the weather, and the time

Timothy Greenfield-Sanders

of day. When asked why she paints these images, Freilicher says, "People often dig so deeply to find the mystery of a painting, and yet it's almost a biological thing—like your posture, or how you sign your name. You just can't do it another way."

ABOUT THE MEDIA
Freilicher paints in oils, makes prints, and designs sets for plays.

ABOUT THE TECHNIQUE
Freilicher's painting technique has been described as bold, with loosely applied colors. She pays close attention to surface textures and the effects of light.

Lorenzo Ghiberti (lō rent´ sō gē bâr´ tē)
(1378 – 1455)

About the Artist

Ghiberti began his career as a goldsmith and a painter in his hometown of Florence, Italy. In 1400, he fled Florence to escape the deadly disease called the plague. However, he soon returned to design a pair of bronze cathedral doors for a contest. The grace and liveliness of the figures in his design helped him win the contest. Ghiberti was still in his early twenties. He became famous almost overnight. He worked on the doors, along with other projects, for more than twenty years.

Ghiberti then produced another set of cathedral doors that took nearly 30 years to complete. Michelangelo called these doors "beautiful enough for the gates of Paradise." Ghiberti's reputation and fortune grew. He married and had two sons, who also became sculptors.

ABOUT ART HISTORY

Ghiberti was one of the great Renaissance artists. He discovered ways to show depth in sculptures, much as paintings show depth. He also wrote a history of ancient art and an autobiography. Ghiberti trained other famous sculptors, including Donatello and Uccello.

ABOUT THE ARTWORK

Ghiberti mainly created religious scenes for cathedrals. Twenty scenes in his doors, for example, are based on biblical stories.

Culver Pictures

ABOUT THE MEDIA

Ghiberti created bronze sculptures and designed stained glass windows.

ABOUT THE TECHNIQUE

Ghiberti's first set of doors consisted of 28 panels. His second set of doors had ten panels. Each panel included raised designs called *reliefs.* The reliefs tell a story. Ghiberti's training as a goldsmith helped him produce accurate details. He covered his second set of doors with gold leaf.

Kathryn Gough (kath´ rin gof)
(1968 –)

About the Artist

Born in Ohio, Gough grew up in a family of artists. Her father, Alan Gough, is a well-known artist who paints landscapes in a naturalistic style. Her mother works in watercolors, and her brother is a photographer. As a child, Gough designed fanciful sets for her marionettes and hand puppets. Her interest in the theater, especially the Ballet Russe, continues. In 1990, Gough earned a bachelor's degree in fine arts at the Columbus College of Art and Design in Ohio. Since then, she has had a number of exhibitions of her work and earned several awards.

Photo courtesy Kathryn Gough

ABOUT ART HISTORY

Gough admires the work of medieval manuscript illustrators, along with that of Pieter Bruegel, Edward Burne-Jones, Gabriel Rossetti, and William Morris.

ABOUT THE ARTWORK

During her college years, Gough painted scenes based on Egyptian myths and theatrical subjects. Now she paints quiet landscapes of the countryside around her rural home. The picture frames she creates for her paintings are often inspired by jewelry and decorative art. After seeing an art artifact in Dublin, Ireland, Gough was fascinated with its design and created a book cover on the same theme. This work, divided into panels with a symmetrical design, varies considerably from her realistic landscapes and shows the range of her skills.

ABOUT THE MEDIA

This artist uses oils, pastels, gesso, and acrylics on paper and on canvas.

ABOUT THE TECHNIQUE

Gough creates frames for her pictures with gesso, a kind of artist's plaster. She forms the gesso into three-dimensional designs that seem to be separate frames. She sometimes glazes small areas of the gesso with acrylics to create imitation enamel and semi-precious stones, much like the medieval manuscripts she admires. In addition, she uses acrylics to suggest gold, silver, and bronze gilding. Real gold, she admits, is "out of my price range right now."

Allan Houser (al´ ən hau´ zər)
(1915 – 1994)

About the Artist

Born in Oklahoma, Houser was the great-nephew of the Apache chief Geronimo. In 1929, he left high school to help out on his family's farm, but he was also able to study his passion—art. In 1936, his paintings were shown at the World's Fair in New York. After he painted several large murals for government buildings in Washington, DC, in 1939 and 1940, he began to explore sculpture. Houser made small wood carvings while he taught art and worked as a pipe fitter's assistant.

Houser's skill and fame grew. In 1946, he created his first large sculpture. It was an eight-foot-tall, four-and-a-half-ton marble piece titled *Comrade in Mourning.* He used only a few hand tools to complete this sculpture honoring the Native Americans who died in World War II. Houser began sculpting full time in 1975. His work has been exhibited and admired throughout the world. He married and had a son who also became a sculptor.

ABOUT ART HISTORY
Houser taught at many schools, including thirteen years at the Institute of American Indian Arts at the Santa Fe Indian School. In this way, he influenced nearly every modern Native American sculptor. With work ranging from realistic to abstract, Houser used art to teach others about Native Americans and to express his pride in his heritage.

ABOUT THE ARTWORK
Most of Houser's subjects were related to his background. Examples include *Offering of the Sacred Pipe, The Future Chiricahua Apache Family,* and a bronze bust of

Jerry Jacka

Geronimo. Houser also illustrated books about Native Americans.

ABOUT THE MEDIA
This artist created sculpture in stone, steel, and bronze. In addition to painting in oils, watercolors, acrylics, and egg tempera, he worked in charcoal and pastels.

ABOUT THE TECHNIQUE
Houser urged his students to search for what satisfied them and then improve whatever they did. He said, "I first please myself. If I don't please myself, no one else will be pleased."

About the Artist

The Athenian statesman Pericles coordinated the rebuilding of the acropolis after the last of Greece's wars with Persia during the middle of the fifth century B.C. Phidias designed and supervised the making of all the sculpture appearing in the Parthenon. Kallikrates began rebuilding the Parthenon on the location of the earlier temple. After the rebuilding of the Parthenon stopped briefly, Pericles commissioned Iktinos to redesign and construct the Parthenon on the existing foundation.

ABOUT ART HISTORY

The Parthenon is a Doric temple–a long, rectangular stone structure with a porch at both ends and surrounded by columns. It also has Ionic elements–thinner and taller columns–and sculptured friezes. A frieze is like a mural carved in stone. The Parthenon stands on the Acropolis, a flat area on a hill that overlooks the Greek city of Athens. Other structures were built at the Acropolis, but none of them were as grand as the Parthenon.

Artist unknown. Parthenon. *447–438 B.C. Marble. 237 × 110 × 60 feet. The Acropolis, Athens, Greece.*

ABOUT THE ARTWORK

The Parthenon was built for the goddess Athena Parthenos. Athena was a warrior-goddess, the daughter of Zeus (the creator of the world in Greek mythology) and the niece of Poseidon (the god of the sea). The Parthenon is like an optical illusion. It looks like a long, tall, rectangular building, but it is really curved and angled. The columns that seem to reach straight up to the sky are actually built at an angle. The frieze around the top of the building shows a celebration honoring Athena. It is 524 feet long. Phidias's statue of Athena, which was made of ivory and more than 2,500 pounds of gold, cost more than the building itself. The Parthenon was used as a temple and later as a storehouse for Turkish ammunition. In 1687, an explosion blew the middle of the structure into pieces.

ABOUT THE MEDIA

The Parthenon was built with white marble, gold, and ivory sculpture. At one time it was painted, but more than time the paint disappeared.

ABOUT THE TECHNIQUE

Building the Parthenon was a giant task. After two years of planning, work began on July 28, 447 B.C. The first year of construction was spent quarrying and moving the white marble from Mount Pentelicus. The superstructure was built between 444–441 B.C. Work on the frieze was also done during this time. In the style of the time, the Parthenon was then covered with gilt (gold) and glass decoration that gave it a shining gold and white appearance.

Yvonne Jacquette (ē von´ jac ket´)
(1934 –   )

About the Artist

Jacquette was born in Pittsburgh. She studied at the Rhode Island School of Design and then moved to New York City. She had her first exhibit in 1965, at the age of 31. She has taught art in colleges and art schools. She is married to filmmaker Rudy Burckhardt and has designed sets for his movies. She and her husband often vacation in Maine. Many of her paintings are Maine landscapes.

ABOUT ART HISTORY

Jacquette was one of the leading painters of American New Realism during the late 1960s. At that time, abstract and pop art were in style. Painting in a realistic style was risky. But Jacquette believes that the lines between realism and abstract art are now blurred. Her art blends the real and the abstract.

ABOUT THE ARTWORK

Jacquette paints landscapes and cityscapes from an overhead point of view, as they appear from a plane. She sometimes includes plane wings in her paintings and titled one painting *The Right Wing II.* Her subjects range from farmlands to tall apartment buildings to industrial sites.

Jacquette often paints night scenes. She shifts around the dots and dashes of light in her paintings to suit herself and to form patterns. Sometimes she uses art to make

Rudy Burkhardt/DC Moore Gallery

order of a jumbled scene, such as Times Square. Some of her paintings show the conflict between people and nature. The possibility of disaster is often a theme. This theme appears in a painting of the Three Mile Island nuclear power plant, for example.

ABOUT THE MEDIA

This artist paints in oils and pastels and creates prints and frescoes. She has also illustrated books.

ABOUT THE TECHNIQUE

Jacquette often works from a penthouse window or a small, circling plane. When she flies in jetliners, she sketches quickly during takeoffs and landings. Sometimes she takes photographs during a flight. She uses them to jog her memory when she returns to her studio and finishes a painting.

Joseph Jean-Gilles (zhō´ zəf zhän zhēl)
(1943–   )

About the Artist

Born in Haiti, Jean-Gilles now lives in Florida, but his native land is never far from his mind. He studied art at Centre d'Art in Port-au-Prince, Haiti, until 1967 and has been painting scenes of his homeland ever since. Jean-Gilles has had a number of exhibitions in New York and Washington, DC, as well as in Haiti. One of his paintings hangs permanently in New York's Museum of Modern Art.

Albert Casciero

ABOUT ART HISTORY
Jean-Gilles is considered a professional primitive painter, much like the nineteenth-century French painter Rousseau. Jean-Gilles has gained skills that take him beyond a spontaneous recording of what he sees or imagines to a carefully planned and sophisticated portrayal of his ideas.

ABOUT THE ARTWORK
Haitian Landscape is an excellent example of Jean-Gilles's art. He paints the tropical landscape of his homeland in an idealized way. For example, his trees differ only slightly in shape, and his human figures are like dolls, almost faceless. This stylized approach makes the painting seem like a fairy tale, which expresses Jean-Gilles's feelings about Haiti. His carefully tended fields show the human influence on the landscape and stress the interdependence of people and nature. With everything in its proper place and nothing amiss, Jean-Gilles reminds viewers that we are all looking for our place in the universe. His ideal view of Haiti, ignoring the reality of the difficult lives of today's Haitians, suggests hope for the future of this politically torn island.

ABOUT THE MEDIA
Jean-Gilles works mainly in oils on canvas.

ABOUT THE TECHNIQUE
In his paintings, Jean-Gilles overlaps objects to show the great variety in the lush landscape. He has studied the trees and plants of Haiti and arranges them into precise patterns. In his design, Jean-Gilles combines vivid colors with interrelated forms.

Isabel John (iz´ ə bel jän)

About the Artist

Isabel John is the best-known weaver of Navajo pictorial rugs today. John probably learned how to weave from an aunt or grandmother. She has been weaving for many years and is now teaching the art to others. She lives on the Navajo reservation in the northeastern Arizona city of Many Farms.

Courtesy, Toh-Atin Gallery

ABOUT ART HISTORY

Weaving is an important part of Navajo culture and history. Isabel John is well known for her pictorial weavings. Pictorial weavings, also known as tapestries, are a recent development in Navajo weaving. Earlier Navajo weavings showed only geometric designs and simple patterns. The earliest example of a Navajo pictorial design was a blanket belonging to a Cheyenne warrior in 1864. This blanket's design was almost completely geometrical but included a bird in each corner. Today's pictorial weavings show images of horses, flags, houses, landscapes, and many other things. Some tell stories about Navajo life.

ABOUT THE ARTWORK

John creates weavings showing scenes from everyday life on the Navajo reservation. She creates visual recordings of the history and traditional ways of the Navajo. Some popular imagery in her artwork includes logos, animals, buildings, road signs, automobiles, trucks, wagons, road signs, and trains. Her weavings are extremely detailed and technically complex.

ABOUT THE MEDIA

Isabel John uses wool from sheep, commercial and natural dyes, and a handmade wooden loom to make her weavings.

ABOUT THE TECHNIQUE

Isabel John shears wool from sheep for her weavings. Then she cards, washes, spins, and dyes the wool. She makes her weavings completely by hand on an upright loom. John starts a weaving with only an idea of how she wants the finished tapestry to look. She does not draw her design on paper before she weaves it. A tapestry can take up to a year to weave.

Calvin Jones (kal´ vin jōnz)
(1934 –   )

About the Artist

Born in Illinois, Jones began exhibiting his work while he was still in elementary school in Chicago. After graduating from high school, he received a full scholarship to the Art Institute of Chicago, where he studied drawing, painting, and illustration. Jones worked for 17 years as an illustrator and graphic designer. He won many awards for his work before deciding to paint full-time. Since then, he has gained widespread recognition for his ability to share the African American experience through modern art.

Photo by Willis Bing Davis

ABOUT ART HISTORY

In his art, Jones combines abstraction with reality. Some of his work involves abstract styles called hard-edge, color-field, and minimal art. These traditional styles from Africa, Asia, and cultures in the Americas were not recognized in the Western world until the twentieth century. They became popular during the 1950s and 1960s. These styles use geometric shapes and colors to express ideas.

ABOUT THE ARTWORK

Jones focuses on abstract images of the African American experience, but his work also stresses that we are all one people. He creates easel paintings and murals that reflect his cultural heritage. Sometimes Jones includes patterns that remind viewers of African textiles, as he did in his painting *Maskamorphosis I.* In this painting, he used symbolic shapes to form masks. His images seem both abstract and realistic.

ABOUT THE MEDIA

Jones works in mixed media, including oils and acrylics.

ABOUT THE TECHNIQUE

This artist combines bright colors and textures with bold designs of intersecting lines and geometric shapes.

Wassily Kandinsky (və sēl´ yē kan din´ skē)
(1866 – 1944)

About the Artist

Wassily Kandinsky first tried painting as a teenager in his native Russia. Even then, he felt that each color had a mysterious life of its own. He was still drawn to colors and painting while he studied law and economics in college. However, at that point he believed that art was "a luxury forbidden to a Russian." In time, though, he moved to Germany, studied art, and began his career. During his life, Kandinsky moved back and forth between Russia and Germany several times. In 1933, he settled in France after Nazi storm troopers labeled his painting style "degenerate."

ABOUT ART HISTORY
Kandinsky was a pioneer in the pure abstract painting style, a combination of color and form with no subject matter. He did not give a title to a painting he did in 1910, but others called it the *First Abstract Watercolour.* Kandinsky felt that trying to paint recognizable objects distracted artists from their real jobs, expressing ideas and emotions. He believed that communicating through painting was similar to communicating with music. He often gave his paintings titles that were both musical and abstract, such as *Improvisation 30.*

ABOUT THE ARTWORK
It's possible to identify landscapes and objects in some of Kandinsky's early

Archiv/Interfoto

paintings, but his later work was entirely abstract. Only occasionally during World War I did Kandinsky include cannons and other recognizable objects in his work.

ABOUT THE MEDIA
Kandinsky worked in oils, watercolors, and India ink.

ABOUT THE TECHNIQUE
Kandinsky did not try to show the "essence" of his subjects, because he had no subjects. Instead, he attempted to make forms and colors take on a meaning that was separate from the physical world. His work often impresses even viewers who are not certain what the paintings are supposed to mean.

Paul Klee (paul klā)
(1879 – 1940)

About the Artist

Klee was born into a musical Swiss family. His family hoped he also would become a musician. At age five, his grandmother gave him his first box of pencils. He thought of himself as an artist from then on. But he kept an interest in music. Klee played his violin for an hour nearly every morning of his life. He married a pianist.

As an adult, Klee drew simply, like a child. Klee believed that childlike drawings were the most creative and original. He was not trying to share his ideas through his work. He simply wanted to explore his imagination. Klee taught himself to paint with both hands.

ABOUT ART HISTORY
At first, art critics ignored Klee's work. Then they realized that Klee's small, charming, playful pictures were filled with ideas and meaning. Different people see different meanings in Klee's pictures. For many people, this fact adds to the value of his pictures.

ABOUT THE ARTWORK
Klee studied nature and often began his pictures with an image from nature. Then he would let his imagination go.

ABOUT THE MEDIA
Klee painted with watercolors and other materials on paper, canvas, silk, linen, and

Culver Pictures

burlap. He liked to experiment. For example, he did one picture with black paste on burlap.

ABOUT THE TECHNIQUE
Color was very important to Klee. He once said, "Color and I are one; I am a painter." In his watercolors, Klee used thin layers of pale color. This technique made his pictures gently shimmer, like pavement under a hot sun. Klee used color like a musician uses sound. He tried to touch viewers' feelings. Klee said that he learned more about painting from the musicians Bach and Mozart than he did from visual artists.

Hughie Lee-Smith (hū´ē lē smith)
(1915–)

About the Artist

Hughie Lee-Smith was born in Eustis, Florida. At an early age, he moved to Cleveland, Ohio. He attended weekend classes at the Cleveland Museum of Art. After high school, he was awarded scholarships to study arts and crafts in Detroit and Cleveland. After college, Lee-Smith went on to teach at a variety of colleges and art centers all over the United States. He moved to New York in the 1970s to be an art instructor at the Art Student's League. During his career, he has earned many awards for his outstanding contributions to art and education. His first retrospective exhibit took place in 1988 when Lee-Smith was 73 years old.

ABOUT ART HISTORY

Lee-Smith's style is deeply rooted in his African American cultural perspective. He draws from romantic realism and surrealism to create his images. He has been compared stylistically with the likes of American artist Edward Hopper and Italian surrealist Giorgio De Chirco.

ABOUT THE ARTWORK

One theme runs through many of Lee-Smith's paintings, loneliness. He uses a sparse landscape where there is a physical and emotional distance between the figures. This distance helps make the viewer aware of underlying themes of isolation and

Manu Sassonian. Courtesy of June Kelly Gallery and VAGA, New York, NY

racial tensions that sometimes arise between people. Lee-Smith's paintings show people's differences and their attempts to get along with each other. The lack of bright color helps to make his message stronger.

ABOUT THE MEDIA

Lee-Smith paints with oils. He is also a printmaker who creates lithographs and etchings.

ABOUT THE TECHNIQUE

Lee-Smith's style is realistic.

Fernand Léger (fer nän´ lā zhā´)
(1881 – 1955)

About the Artist

Léger's parents were French peasants, but his art strayed far from the rural countryside. He spent his life exploring the modern industrial world from an artist's point of view. Perhaps his early training in an architect's office encouraged his fascination with what came to be known as "machine art."

Archive Photos

ABOUT ART HISTORY

Léger was strongly influenced by Cézanne and became a cubist painter. Like other cubists, Léger looked at his subjects from several angles and combined the angles in the same picture. For example, he might show the top, bottom, and sides of a subject in one painting. To do this, cubists broke a subject into surfaces or "planes." To some people, cubist paintings seem to be cubes or boxes falling through space.

Léger combined the cubist painting style with images from the industrial world. The people in his pictures, broken into flat planes, seem more like robots than humans. Léger often showed buildings as cones and cylinders that looked like machine parts. Toward the end of Léger's life, his art became increasingly abstract and geometric.

ABOUT THE ARTWORK

One of Léger's favorite subjects was the city. He was fascinated by the combined effects of large billboards, flashing lights, noisy traffic, and the movement of people. Léger also painted people in motion in two series called *The Divers* and *The Cyclists.* In addition, he used the cubist style to paint circus scenes and family picnics.

ABOUT THE MEDIA

Besides creating oil paintings, Léger designed sets for ballets and motion pictures. He also worked in ceramics, stained glass, and mosaics.

ABOUT THE TECHNIQUE

In his early paintings, Léger used bright colors and heavy black outlines, like a poster. Later, he painted abstract color patterns and drew outlined subjects over them.

Nancy Youngblood Lugo

(nan´ sē yung´ blud lū´ gō)   *(1955 –   )*

About the Artist

Youngblood Lugo was born in Fort Lewis, Washington. Her mother is Native American and her father is of English and Scottish descent. Her father was in the military, so they moved many times. She has lived on and off in Santa Clara, New Mexico, since she was 12. At a very early age, she wanted to be an artist. She went to the San Francisco Art Institute on a scholarship. Later, she worked in a Native American art gallery. The owner, Al Packard, encouraged her to follow in her family's footsteps. She had her first major show when she was 20. Youngblood Lugo still lives in Santa Clara and has three sons. She says that each work, which she never rushes to finish, surprises and challenges her.

ABOUT ART HISTORY

Southwest potters have been using the same clay and methods for centuries. Youngblood Lugo is part of a long tradition of well-known potters called the Tafoya family. Her grandmother was Margaret Tafoya.

ABOUT THE ARTWORK

Although Youngblood Lugo has continued to use traditional southwest Native American styles in her work, she manages to make each piece distinctly hers. She continues the traditional black matte finishes, and incorporates designs like seashells into surfaces made of caramel-colored slip. All show the natural, rich colors from the earth.

ABOUT THE MEDIA

Youngblood Lugo digs the clay from hills around Santa Clara. She prepares the clay through a long, painstaking process that can take several months.

Copyright © 1996, The Heard Museum (Phoenix, AZ)/Photo by Tamea Mikesell

ABOUT THE TECHNIQUE

Youngblood Lugo rolls the clay into long coils, around and around into a pot shape. With her fingers, she smears the coils into each other to form the sides of the pot. When the pot feels leather hard but not too dry, she starts carving. Then the pot needs to finish drying. This can take up to ten months. Youngblood Lugo puts the pot into a bag for a few hours a day so that it will not dry too quickly. After this stage, she sands the pot with sandpaper. Later, she applies a colored slip and then, after the pot dries, she polishes it with a smooth stone. She fires her pots at the Pueblo reservation where she built a firing shed that she says looks like a Kentucky Fried Chicken restaurant. Each piece is fired separately.

Man Ray (man rā)
(1890 – 1976)

About the Artist

Man Ray was born in Philadelphia. His parents named him Emanuel Rabinovitch. After studying architecture and engineering, he turned to painting. Ray married a French painter and eventually moved to Paris. To support himself, he took photographs of friends' paintings and of French celebrities. In time, Ray combined photography and painting by placing objects on photographically sensitive paper. He called the resulting image a "Rayograph." A Rayograph was a pattern of shadows and tones rather than a photograph. Ray and his wife moved back and forth between Paris and the United States several times. He continued to paint and try new techniques until his death at age 86.

ABOUT ART HISTORY

Ray and his wife helped found the Dada movement in New York. This movement was named by opening a dictionary and choosing a word at random. Dadaist artists were critical of painting styles and made fun of them. The Dada movement was actually a revolt against artistic styles. Ray himself purposely tried to paint not only unlike other artists, but even unlike his own earlier paintings. After the Rays moved to Paris, they joined the Surrealist movement, which tried to find new relationships between unlikely objects. For example, one of Ray's surrealist paintings is a huge pair of lips resting against a sunset.

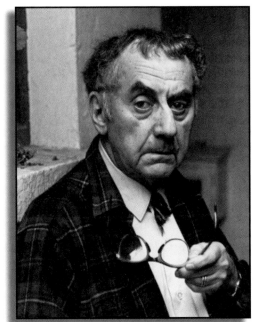

Corbis

ABOUT THE ARTWORK

Along with paintings and photography, Ray produced films and what he called "ready-mades." "Ready-mades" were commercially made objects that were sold as art. One of Ray's "ready-mades" was an old-fashioned iron, painted black. He had metal tacks attached to the bottom with the points facing outward. He meant to surprise people with his odd combination of materials.

ABOUT THE TECHNIQUE

Ray was constantly experimenting with new painting and photography techniques. In one of his photographs, he gave a woman three sets of eyes. Along with his Rayographs, he tried painting on glass with an airbrush.

Sylvia Plimack Mangold
(sil´ vē ə pli´ mak man´ gōld) *(1938 –   )*

About the Artist

Mangold was born in New York City. She attended several art schools and earned a degree in fine arts from Yale University. In 1974, she had her first show. Her work has been much admired ever since. Mangold teaches at the School of Visual Arts in New York City. She is married to artist Robert Mangold, and they have two sons. She lives on a 150-acre farm in Washingtonville, New York.

Courtesy of Alexander and Bonin, NY. Photo by Peter Bellamy

ABOUT ART HISTORY
Mangold's work has been called realistic. However, her work does not fit easily into a category. Her realistic paintings still have an abstract quality.

ABOUT THE ARTWORK
Mangold paints her surroundings. Early in her career, she painted floors and rooms. Later, she painted scenes outside the studio window on her farm. Since 1983, Mangold has painted landscapes around her home. She has made many paintings of trees. She often makes one tree the focus of a painting.

ABOUT THE MEDIA
Mangold works in oils on canvas and linen and in watercolors, acrylics, pencil, ink, and pastels. She also creates prints.

ABOUT THE TECHNIQUE
Mangold tries to make her paintings seem three-dimensional, like sculpture. She uses rulers and masking tape in creating her paintings. She includes these tools in some of her pictures. For example, Mangold sometimes uses masking tape to define the borders in landscape paintings. She often leaves the used tape on the canvas, as part of the picture. Mangold usually sketches her subjects outdoors and completes the paintings in her studio.

About the Artist

Henri Matisse was the son of a middle-class couple in the north of France. He was not interested in art while he was in school. After high school, his father sent him to law school in Paris. When he was 21, an appendicitis attack changed his life. Because he had to spend a long time in the hospital, his mother brought him a paint box to help him pass the time. Matisse eventually convinced his father to let him drop out of law school and study art.

Matisse married and soon had a family. His paintings weren't selling, so he worked for a decorator and his wife opened a hat shop. During his last years of life, he sufferd from arthritis. Unable to hold a brush in his hands, he devoted his efforts to making paper cutouts from papers painted to his specifications and created fantastic, brightly colored shapes. Unlike many other artists, he was internationally famous during his lifetime.

ABOUT ART HISTORY

In 1905, Matisse exhibited with his friends in a painting style showing strong emotionalism, wild colors, and distortion of shape. They were called *les fauves,* or the wild beasts. They experimented with intense, sometimes violent colors. Without letting their work become abstract, Matisse and other Fauve painters tested the bounds of reality.

ABOUT THE ARTWORK

Matisse painted still lifes, room interiors, and landscapes. His paintings of dancers and human figures were generally more concerned with expressive shape than accurate representation of anatomy.

UPI/Corbis-Bettmann

At one time, he was asked to design a chapel. He designed the entire structure, including the stained-glass windows and the vestments for the priests.

ABOUT THE MEDIA

Matisse painted primarily with oils. He created many prints. Later in life, he worked with cut paper.

ABOUT THE TECHNIQUE

Matisse worked with bold, intense colors. He simplified and distorted shapes for expressive qualities. He was more interested in the way the visual elements were organized than in realistic representation.

Michelangelo (mi kəl an´ jə lō)
(1475–1564)

About the Artist

Michelangelo Buonarroti was born in the mountain village of Caprese, Italy. Even at an early age, his talent for drawing was obvious. His father, a Florentine official who was connected to the ruling Medici family, apprenticed his son to the master painter, Ghirlandaio. After two years, Michelangelo attended the sculpture school sponsored by the Medici family. Michelangelo was introduced to the leaders of France by Lorenzo de' Medici. When Lorenzo died, Michelangelo fled to Rome where he examined many newly unearthed classical statues. In 1505, he was recalled to Rome and given two commissions by the Pope—A Tomb for Julius II, and the painting of the ceiling of the Sistine Chapel. It took him four years to cover the ceiling with fresco painting. The Pope had him complete the Sistine chapel by covering the alter wall with a fresco, *The Last Judgement*.

Michelangelo turned to architecture late in his life. He was made chief architect in charge of rebuilding St. Peter's Basilica. The dome he designed has become the model for domes all over the western world.

ABOUT ART HISTORY

Michelangelo was one of the most inspired creators in the history of art, and with Leonardo da Vinci, the leading force in the Italian High Renaissance. He was a sculptor, architect, painter, and poet. He had a tremendous influence on his contemporaries and on all the Western European art that followed.

Superstock

ABOUT THE ARTWORK

Like other artists of his time, Michelangelo focused on religious topics. Among his timeless works of art are the ceiling of the Sistine Chapel, the statue of *David*, his painting *The Last Judgment*, and the design of St. Peter's Basilica.

ABOUT THE MEDIA

Michelangelo carved magnificent marble statues. He painted using a fresco technique.

ABOUT THE TECHNIQUE

After making many plans, Michelangelo carved directly into the marble using chisels and finishing tools. For his fresco paintings, he first drew "cartoons" and transferred the image to the wall or ceiling before painting. Plaster was applied only to the area that would be painted that day. Pigment was mixed with water and applied directly onto the wet plaster The color would then become part of the plaster, remaining as bright as when it was applied.

Ayako Miyawaki (ä ē kō mē yä wä kē)
(1905 –   )

About the Artist

During World War II, Japanese artist Miyawaki spent much of her time in bomb shelters. As soon as the war ended, she began to experiment with fabric art. She had never attended art school. She used old clothes and rags to show her ideas. She created her first fabric picture, called *appliqué,* in 1945 at age 40. In 1950, she had her first public exhibit—in a candy store. Since then, her work has become very popular. It is exhibited in Japan and the United States. Her husband was a teacher and painter, and they had several children.

ABOUT ART HISTORY

Miyawaki's work followed a long tradition in Japanese art. It focused on showing appreciation for the beauty all around. Appliqué is an ancient art. People probably created appliqué as early as 200 B.C. Miyawaki's technique of using string in her appliqué also dates back to ancient times.

ABOUT THE ARTWORK

Miyawaki pictured objects from nature, such as fish, fruit, flowers, and vegetables, in her designs. One of her appliqués, *The Red Crab,* combines red and green fabric of smooth and rough textures. The design seems both ancient and playful.

Hiroshi Okuda

ABOUT THE MEDIA

Appliqué is also called "rag art." Appliqué artists combine pieces of fabric to make pictures and designs. Miyawaki used brightly colored fabrics with Japanese designs. Sometimes she dyed worn fabric into the vivid colors she liked.

ABOUT THE TECHNIQUE

Miyawaki worked without using patterns. She cut fabric pieces freehand and sewed or glued them onto her canvas. She often combined different textures. She also used the threads that attached the pieces of fabric as part of her design. In many works, the fabric pieces look like splashes of paint on a canvas.

Claude Monet (klōd mō nā´)
(1840 – 1926)

About the Artist

As a young man in France, Claude Monet did not want to be a painter. He already was well paid for drawing caricatures of tourists. However, painter Eugene Boudin saw talent in Monet's exaggerated drawings and encouraged him to paint. Although artists were "supposed" to paint in studios, Boudin urged Monet to paint outside in the open air. There, Monet learned to capture his first impressions on canvas. He recorded these impressions during a long and productive life, outliving two wives. His greatest wish was to "mingle more closely with nature." By his death at 86, Monet was blinded by cataracts.

ABOUT ART HISTORY

Monet made a large contribution to the development of Impressionism through his ideas and painting. Unlike most painters before him, Monet painted outdoors. He made careful observations of subject matter, studying the changes in appearance due to light and weather. In the first Impressionist exhibition, Monet included a work titled *Impression, Sunrise.* A critic, ridiculing the colors, strange distortion of shapes, and loose brush strokes, derived the name *Impressionism* from this title. The term *Impressionism* was soon accepted and used by the public to describe this new style of painting.

ABOUT THE ARTWORK

Monet painted landscapes and people, but he especially loved scenes that included water. At one time, he had a floating studio: he filled a rowboat with art supplies and painted in the

Archive Photos

shade of a striped awning. Toward the end of his life, Monet painted huge landscapes of the garden and lily ponds near his home in Giverny, France.

ABOUT THE MEDIA

Although he made sketches later in life, Monet created mostly oil paintings. By the 1870s, Monet eliminated black from his palette, replacing it with blue.

ABOUT THE TECHNIQUE

Monet often began a painting by covering the canvas with a background color. Then, he dabbed paint here and there until shapes became recognizable. He was fascinated by the way the same color could look different at certain times of the day or during particular weather conditions. He often painted the same subjects over and over again to capture this in his paintings. Examples of motifs he painted many times include Rouen Cathedral, poplars, haystacks, and water lilies.

34

Henry Moore (hen´ rē môr)
(1898 – 1986)

About the Artist

Moore was born in Castleford, England. When he was 10 years old, he told his father he wanted to become a sculptor. At the age of 18, he left home to join the army during World War I. After the war, he began studying art. By the age of 23, he was a serious sculptor. Moore felt that his ability to do the hard physical labor required for sculpting large pieces came from his mother.

© *Photo by Rollie McKenna/Photo Researchers, Inc.*

ABOUT ART HISTORY

In the 1930s, many sculptors were producing realistic works. But Moore and a few of his artist friends started creating sculpture that was more abstract. Moore simplified human figures and emphasized curving forms. He also used holes in his sculptures, which he associated with the mystery of caves. His early works show the influence of Mexican and African carvings. Many critics consider Moore the greatest English sculptor of the 1900s.

ABOUT THE ARTWORK

Moore frequently combined his figures with shapes and textures from nature. He focused on making the simplest form of the subject he carved. Moore thought of his large sculptures as part of the open air with the sky as the background. Families were an important subject of his sculptures. His own family inspired his work.

ABOUT THE MEDIA

Moore carved some sculptures in wood and some in stone. He used bronze for most of his large sculptures.

ABOUT THE TECHNIQUE

Moore collected pebbles; flints; shells; animal bones; and old, weathered pieces of wood for his studio. These pieces spurred him on to draw. From his sketches, he made small models for his sculptures. Then he made larger models. After much planning, he was ready to make the actual sculptures.

About the Artist

Noguchi was born in Los Angeles, grew up in Japan, and went to high school in Indiana. His mother was an American writer and his father was a Japanese poet. After an art instructor discouraged him from becoming a sculptor, Noguchi studied medicine for a while. But he returned to sculpture. At his first exhibition in 1929, no one bought any of his work. To support himself, Noguchi turned to portrait painting. He also studied brush drawing and pottery in China and Japan. He then went to New York and designed playgrounds, theater sets, portrait busts, murals, and a fountain. During World War II, Noguchi voluntarily spent six months in a Japanese internment camp, designing recreation areas that were never built. After studying art in England, Europe, and Asia, he began to design public plazas and gardens. Noguchi called his work "sculpture of spaces."

ABOUT ART HISTORY

Noguchi's work is an abstract combination of Eastern and Western art. His style was influenced by artists Alfred Stieglitz, J. B. Neumann, and Constantin Brancusi as well as by Japanese stoneworkers. Noguchi did not create art for the sake of art; he wanted his creations to be usable and meaningful.

ABOUT THE ARTWORK

One of Noguchi's best-known sculpture gardens is located at Yale University. Created in white marble, *Sunken Garden* includes a pyramid and a cube balancing on one point. Other examples of his work include *Garden of Peace* at the UNESCO

Nathan Benn/Woodfin Camp & Associates

headquarters in Paris and *Children's Land*, a playground near Tokyo.

ABOUT THE MEDIA

The materials Noguchi used varied from project to project. Although he often used terra-cotta clay or stainless steel, he is most famous for his use of stone. He traveled worldwide and even climbed mountains to find the right stones for his sculptures.

ABOUT THE TECHNIQUE

Much of Noguchi's work consists of abstract, rounded forms in polished stone. In some pieces, he used enormous blocks of stone, which he gouged and hammered.

Pablo Picasso (pä´ blō pē käs´ sō)
(1881 – 1973)

About the Artist

Picasso was born in Spain. He did poorly in school, but his father, an art teacher, taught him to draw and paint. Picasso learned quickly. When he was only 14, he had a painting accepted for an exhibition. Picasso moved to Paris when he was 18. At the time, he was very poor. Once, thieves stole what little he had, yet they left his now valuable drawings. In time, the outgoing Picasso made many friends. Among them were the American writers Ernest Hemingway and Gertrude Stein and the Russian composer Igor Stravinsky. Picasso painted at night and slept late most mornings. He worked hard his entire life. He completed two hundred paintings the year he turned ninety.

ABOUT ART HISTORY

Picasso was the most influential artist of the 1900s. He experimented with many styles and created new ones. He invented the style known as Cubism. He took 18 months to paint his first cubist picture, *Les Demoiselles d'Avignon.* It shows five women from several angles. Soon, other artists were copying his style.

ABOUT THE ARTWORK

Picasso's paintings changed as his life changed. When he was poor, he painted sad pictures in shades of blue. This style is called the *Blue Period.* When he fell in love with a neighbor, he painted happier pictures in shades of pink. This style is called the *Rose Period.* Then came his

Self-Portrait. *Philadelphia Museum of Art. A. E. Gallatin Collection. © 1998 Estate of Pablo Picasso/Artist Rights Society (ARS), New York. Photo by Graydon Wood.*

cubist period, and later he painted in a style that reminded viewers of Greek sculpture.

ABOUT THE MEDIA

Picasso created drawings, oil paintings, ceramic pieces, sculpture, prints, and engravings. He also invented collage along with the French artist Georges Braque. They combined colored papers, newspaper, old illustrations, and small objects with painting and drawing to produce collages.

ABOUT THE TECHNIQUE

In his cubist paintings, Picasso simplified his subjects into circles, triangles, and other basic shapes. He often outlined these shapes in black or a bright color.

Horace Pippin (hôr əs pip´ ən)
(1888 – 1946)

About the Artist

Pippin was born to a poor woman in Pennsylvania. As a child, he sketched in pencil and crayon. At school, he drew all his spelling words. Then he had to stay after school to do the lesson again, the "right" way. Later, he worked in a feed store, a coal yard, a hotel, and a factory. When World War I began, Pippin joined the army. He was sent to France in 1917. A bullet wounded his right arm and left it limp. Pippin was sent home, but he could no longer draw well. Instead, he learned to create designs with a hot poker on boards. After a time, he gained some control over his arm and was able to paint again. Pippin took a few art classes late in his life. But he decided that art could not be taught. On his own, he mastered color and design.

ABOUT ART HISTORY

As a folk artist, Pippin used simple designs and colors to express complex ideas. In 1937, an art collector saw one of Pippin's paintings in a shoemaker's shop in Pennsylvania. A year later, Pippin's work hung in New York's Museum of Modern Art. The exhibit was titled "Masters of Popular Painting." Pippin's great talent was finally recognized. Soon many art museums wanted a "Pippin."

ABOUT THE ARTWORK

Pippin first painted his war experiences. Then he painted the everyday lives of African Americans from his childhood memories. His work included portraits, still lifes, and

©1945 Arnold Newman

biblical scenes. He also painted scenes from African American history, such as *John Brown Going to His Hanging.*

ABOUT THE MEDIA

Pippin began his career by burning designs into wood with a hot poker. He later worked with oils on canvas.

ABOUT THE TECHNIQUE

For most of his life, Pippin painted in a small room in his home. For light, he had one shadeless lightbulb. He sometimes worked for seventeen hours straight. He painted the images in his mind with carefully chosen colors.

Rosalind Ragans (roz´ ə lind rā´ gənz)
(1933 –   )

About the Artist

Ragans was born and grew up in New York City. When she was 11 years old, polio paralyzed her right side. Fortunately, two years of therapy helped her regain nearly all the movement she had lost. Ragans had planned to be a stage designer but discovered that she loved teaching art. She began teaching in New Jersey in 1956. She earned a doctoral degree in education. While teaching art in Georgia in 1975, she began developing *ArtTalk.* This art education program presents art as a language, or a way of communicating. Since 1980, Ragans has been afflicted by post-polio syndrome, which has made walking difficult. Still, she continues to work on *ArtTalk*. Published in 1987, it has been well received by art teachers across the nation. Since then, Ragans has created *Art Connections,* which you are using now. She still finds time to create the batik paintings she loves.

ABOUT ART HISTORY
Ragans works in a style of her own that approaches abstraction. Like two artists she admires, Alice Neel and Frida Kahlo, she uses her art to deal with personal conflicts. For example, her *Self Portrait*, subtitled "My Soul Dances," expresses her mind's ability to dance even though her body cannot.

ABOUT THE ARTWORK
All of Ragans's batik paintings have dancers and plants in them, either as the main subject or hidden in the background. Ragans has always loved music and dancing. She is fascinated by plants because she saw so few of them as a child in New York City.

Rosalind Ragans

ABOUT THE MEDIA
Ragans uses dyes and untreated rayon, cotton, linen, and silk to create her batiks.

ABOUT THE TECHNIQUE
After sketching an image on fabric, Ragans uses hot wax to cover the areas she wants to remain white. Then, she applies the colors, beginning with the palest ones. After each color dries, she covers it with hot wax so that it will not be affected by later colors. The last step is removing most of the wax with paper towels and an iron. Any remaining wax adds a glow to the image.

About the Artist

Frederic Remington was born in Canton, New York, in 1861. He was a horse and nature lover as a child. These loves became the subjects of his art. He studied at Yale University from 1878 to 1880. In 1881, he made his first trip to the American West and felt that it was about to vanish forever. He sold some of the drawings he made on this trip to *Harper's Weekly.* This started his career as an illustrator. He made trips to the West every year to gather material for his drawings. In 1885, he decided to become a painter, devoting his work to showing the rapidly vanishing culture of the cowboys and Native Americans of the West. Before his death in 1909, Remington successfully turned to sculpture.

ABOUT ART HISTORY

Remington is best known for his depiction of the West. Done in a typically realist style, Remington's illustrations were widely successful. His drawings of the Spanish-American War recorded the swift action of events with accuracy and attention to detail. Realistic depiction was characteristic of the work of many American artists at that time.

ABOUT THE ARTWORK

Remington's subjects were drawn from his life on the Western plains. They include cowboys, Native Americans, soldiers, and horses. He produced oils, drawings, illustrations, and bronzes.

Self-Portrait on a Horse. *Sid Richardson Collection of Western Art.*

ABOUT THE TECHNIQUE

Remington spent most of his time in the East. He worked from sketches and photographs from his trips west. He also collected props, such as saddles, bows and arrows, and moccasins that he used as models. When drawing in his studio, he carefully arranged these elements into his work. He always paid close attention to composition.

About the Artist

French artist Rigaud learned to paint from a relative. By 1682, he had enough skill to win a major prize from Italy's Royal Academy of Art. The prize would have paid for him to study at the academy. However, Rigaud turned it down and opened a studio in Paris instead. His career took off in 1688, after he painted a portrait of the French king's brother.

ABOUT ART HISTORY

Rigaud was influenced by the style of portrait painting done by the Dutch painter Rembrandt. But Rigaud himself painted in a baroque style. He portrayed his subjects as serious, stately, and formal. He framed them in rich and elegant surroundings. During his lifetime, Rigaud was very much in demand as a portrait painter. Many religious and political leaders had their portraits painted by him.

ABOUT THE ARTWORK

Rigaud became famous for his portraits, especially *The Sun King.* He completed it in 1701. It shows Louis XIV in all his glory. The king is dressed in ermine- and gold-trimmed robes. He is showing off his legs, of which he was proud. Louis liked this portrait so much that he ordered Rigaud to paint a second one. Rigaud and his staff completed 30 to 40

Laura Platt Winfrey/
Woodfin Camp & Associates

portraits a year. They painted kings from France, Sweden, Spain, and Poland.

ABOUT THE MEDIA

Rigaud worked in oils on canvas.

ABOUT THE TECHNIQUE

Rigaud was skilled in showing off his subjects' best features and playing down their weaknesses. This skill made him a popular portrait painter. He paid careful attention to the details in his subjects' costumes and their surroundings. Rigaud directed a workshop of artists. Some of Rigaud's assistants were especially good at painting draperies or other parts of the portraits. Sometimes, Rigaud added only the head to a figure painted by his assistants. Other times, he simply added some finishing touches and signed the portrait.

Faith Ringgold (fāth ring´ gōld)
(1930 –   )

About the Artist

Ringgold grew up in Harlem in New York City. As a child, her asthma often kept her home from school. To pass the time, her mother taught her how to draw and sew. After high school, Ringgold wanted to become an artist, but at the time, the City College of New York did not allow women to study liberal arts. So Ringgold became an art teacher and taught for almost 20 years. She used her own artwork to draw attention to the challenges faced by African Americans, especially women.

By the 1980s, people had started to notice and admire her work. Today, she is a respected artist who is still finding new ways to express her feelings.

ABOUT ART HISTORY
Ringgold has helped make African art popular in the United States. She has also promoted the use of fabric art.

ABOUT THE ARTWORK
Ringgold focuses on the lives of African Americans. Her work ranges from cloth portraits of individuals to quilted squares that tell stories.

ABOUT THE MEDIA
At first, Ringgold worked in oils, watercolors, and acrylics. Then a student suggested that Ringgold do what she taught her students to do—work with traditional African materials. Ringgold now creates life-size cloth masks of such people as her aunts

Photo by C'Love

and the Rev. Martin Luther King, Jr. The masks are attached to clothing and can be worn like costumes.

Ringgold also makes quilts and soft-sculpture people from stuffed stockings. Her quilts tell stories, with and without words. *Church Picnic,* for example, shows how a minister and a young woman fell in love. Sometimes Ringgold combines her quilts with singing and dancing to tell stories.

ABOUT THE TECHNIQUE
Ringgold uses bright colors and bold patterns to show the energy in the African American community.

Diego Rivera (dē ā′ gō rē bā′ rä)
(1886 – 1957)

About the Artist

Rivera was one of the most productive Mexican artists. He attended art school in Mexico but did not stay long. His first exhibition of paintings in 1907 won him a scholarship to Europe. There, he studied the work of modern artists. After returning from a second trip to Europe in 1911, he became Mexico's leading mural painter. Rivera was a large man with strong opinions. His great love for his people and his country showed in his art. Crowds gathered to watch him paint his large murals on public walls. His third wife was the famous painter Frida Kahlo. They often fought and separated, but they always supported each other's artistic efforts.

ABOUT ART HISTORY

Rivera's painting style was influenced by the work of Klee, Cézanne, Picasso, and other modern painters. Rivera wanted to create art that could be enjoyed and understood by ordinary people. For this reason, he focused on simple designs and interesting subjects. Public murals were ideal for him because many people could see his art.

ABOUT THE ARTWORK

Rivera painted more than two-and-one-half miles of murals in Mexico, San Francisco, Detroit, and New York. For a huge stairway at the National Palace in Mexico City, Rivera painted 124 panels. The panels trace the history of Mexico. In his

Library of Congress/Corbis

other murals, Rivera often showed peasants working or celebrating.

ABOUT THE MEDIA

Rivera completed about 300 frescoes, which are paintings on fresh, moist plaster. Rivera also painted on canvas with oils and watercolors.

ABOUT THE TECHNIQUE

For his frescoes, Rivera drew his designs on the damp plaster and then copied them on transparent paper. If the plaster dried out before Rivera could complete the painting, his assistant used the paper to trace the designs back on the wall.

Auguste Rodin (ō gūst rō dan)
(1840–1917)

About the Artist

Rodin was born to the son of a police officer in Paris. He dominated the world of sculpture at the end of the nineteenth century and the beginning of the twentieth century. He studied art in a free school for artisans and on his own at the Louvre. He was refused admittance to the École des Beaux-Arts. For many years he worked for other sculptors. In 1875, he traveled to Italy, where he was strongly influenced by the works of the Renaissance sculptors Donatello and Michelangelo. After viewing their work, he began to produce intensely muscular figures in unusual poses. Rodin first gained recognition in 1877 for his male figure, *The Age of Bronze*, when it was exhibited at the Salon. The work was so realistic that some critics accused him of making plaster casts from living models. His status as the leading sculptor in France was confirmed in 1884, when he won a competition for representing an incident from the Hundred Years War with his sculpture, *The Burghers of Calais*.

ABOUT ART HISTORY
Rodin was an individual, but he has been classified by some historians with the Impressionists because he was able to capture the most fleeting moments of life. Other historians see him as a post-Impressionist. His most popular work is *The Thinker*.

ABOUT THE ARTWORK
Rodin believed that beauty in art required the truthful representation of inner emotions, and to express this he often distorted anatomy in subtle manipulations. If you ever see his sculpture *The Thinker* you will notice that the figure is twisted slightly into an impossible pose, making the figure more expressive. Rodin's sculpture has two styles. The first is a deliberate roughness of form

Culver Pictures

and surface. His second style is marked by a polished, smooth surface and a delicate form.

ABOUT THE MEDIA
Rodin worked in bronze and marble.

ABOUT THE TECHNIQUE
Rodin's sculpture technique was similar to the Impressionists' painting technique. He added pieces of clay or wax to his forms bit by bit, just as the painters added dots and dashes of paint to their canvases. This makes light and dark play over the uneven surface of his sculptures, giving them a quality of life and vitality. Rodin had his models walk around the studio so that he could observe their bodies as they moved.

Shirley Russell (shûr´ lē rəs´ əl)
(1886 – 1985)

About the Artist

Russell was born in California and studied art in college. The turning point of her career was a trip to Hawaii with her husband in 1921. Not long afterward, her husband died. Russell returned to Hawaii in 1923 and taught art at a high school for the next 23 years. Two of her students became prominent artists. Russell also studied art in Paris from 1927 to 1928 and from 1937 to 1938 to build her own creative skills. Her work has been exhibited not only in Hawaii, but also in Los Angeles, San Francisco, Cincinnati, New York, and Baltimore.

ABOUT ART HISTORY

Like many Hawaiian artists, Russell painted the life around her. She might be considered part of the Hawaiian Modern school of painting, which existed from 1894 to 1941. This group of artists, some residents and some visitors, recorded their interpretations of Hawaii using modern painting styles.

ABOUT THE ARTWORK

Russell concentrated on seascapes, landscapes, and still lifes. One of her well-known paintings is titled *Boys' Day.*

*Courtesy John P. Russell/
Photograph by Herbert Bauer*

It shows what was once an annual Hawaiian celebration held in plantation camps and in the Asian section of towns. The celebration featured long streamers of brightly colored paper carp hung from poles and rooftops. By swimming upstream, carp persisted in the face of overwhelming odds. The village elders thought they offered a good model for young boys.

ABOUT THE MEDIA

This artist worked mainly in oils on canvas.

Rachel Ruysch (rā´ chəl rois)
(1664 – 1750)

About the Artist

Although she lived in Holland during the seventeenth and eighteenth centuries, Ruysch was a modern woman. During her lifetime, few women worked outside the home. Fewer still worked in the arts. Yet Ruysch became a successful artist, encouraged by both her parents and her husband. She had great talent, and her paintings sold quickly. In fact, her pictures cost more than those by another Dutch artist who lived at the same time—Rembrandt. Ruysch also found time to raise her ten children. She continued to paint well past her eightieth birthday.

ABOUT ART HISTORY
Ruysch's paintings are excellent examples of realism. Her father was a botanist, a scientist who studied plants. Perhaps he influenced her to include precise and accurate details in her paintings of flowers and fruit. Ruysch sometimes showed the complete blooming cycle of a flower, from bud to falling petals, in one bouquet. She added other realistic features by including crawling and flying insects in her paintings.

ABOUT THE ARTWORK
During the seventeenth and eighteenth centuries, the Dutch people were fascinated with flowers. This

Rachel Ruysch. (Dutch). Roses, Convolvulus, Poppies and Other Flowers in an Urn on a Stone Ledge. *c. 1745. Oil on canvas. 42½ × 33 inches. The National Museum of Women in the Arts, Washington, DC, Gift of Wallace and Wilhelmina Holladay.*

interest led them to develop many new varieties of tulips and other flowers. Ruysch, too, focused on flowers. She blended science, nature, and art in her paintings.

ABOUT THE MEDIA
Ruysch produced hundreds of oil paintings.

ABOUT THE TECHNIQUE
This artist was patient and careful. She took as long as seven years to complete three paintings. Ruysch painted each petal of every flower separately. However, her lively designs and contrasting colors gave movement and energy to her paintings.

Iris Sandkühler (ī´ ris sand´ kū lər)
(1958 –   )

About the Artist

Iris Sandkühler was born in Bingen, West Germany. Her family emigrated to the United States when she was 12 years old. She became an American citizen five years later. Her mother was very interested in antiques and often gave her jewelry as presents. In college, she studied glassblowing. She also became qualified to teach jewelry design. She teaches full time at Georgia Southern University and continues to make jewelry, sculpture, and artist's books.

ABOUT ART HISTORY

In the past, jewelry was worn as personal adornment, for religious purposes, or to show a person's rank or nobility. People who create jewelry may concentrate on metalworking, gem cutting, or making glass plates. The most common forms of jewelry are necklaces, earrings, bracelets, and rings. In prehistoric times, these items were made of pebbles, bones, and animal teeth and antlers. After the invention of metalworking, metal and stones could be combined in jewelry pieces.

ABOUT THE ARTWORK

Iris Sandkühler's jewelry echoes the beaches on which she finds some of the glass she uses. The copper pendants she makes are made through a process called electroforming. These pendants have organic, natural shapes. The chains Sandkühler makes to complement her pendants are delicate and fine and may remind the viewer of moss.

Photo courtesy Iris Sandkühler

ABOUT THE MEDIA

Some of the glass Sandkühler uses is left over from glassblowing. She also collects beach glass. Beach glass is shards of glass worn smooth by the sand and water of the ocean. Sandkühler's settings and chains are made of copper, brass, or sterling. Sandkühler uses a special device called a rectifier for copper electroforming. She also uses pliers to create her chains and polishing wheels to smooth the rough texture of her copper electroforming.

ABOUT THE TECHNIQUE

For Sandkühler, jewelry making is a meditative process. She is inspired by shards of glass left over from glassblowing or found on the beach. When she works with copper, the electroforming can be unpredictable and sometimes she spends hours polishing rough areas. Making chains is very time-consuming and repetitive, but Sandkühler finds it relaxing.

Tommye Scanlin (tom´ē skan´lin)
(1947 –   )

About the Artist

Tommye Scanlin was born in Georgia. She received her degree in art from the University of Georgia. Although her concentration was in painting, printmaking, and drawing, she felt that something was missing from her artistic experience. While working as a high school art teacher, Scanlin claims that a voice inside her told her that her artistic calling was in weaving. She began reading about and researching weaving. She built her first loom soon after and has been weaving for the past 18 years. She is an active member in several national weaving guilds.

ABOUT ART HISTORY
Weaving is one of the world's oldest art forms. Almost every area of the world has its own special contribution to the art form.

ABOUT THE ARTWORK
Most of Tommye Scanlin's weavings are hanging pieces. Her true love is creating tapestries. Tapestries are weavings that include designs and pictures within the weaving pattern. Scanlin uses a special kind of wool called Spelsau that comes from a primitive breed

Courtesy of Tommye Scanlin

of sheep in Norway. Her work hangs in banks and private home collections.

ABOUT THE MEDIA
Scanlin works with wool and natural fibers.

ABOUT THE TECHNIQUE
Tapestry is the principal form of pictorial weaving. This process is much slower than normal loom weaving. Large tapestries can be woven on either a vertical or a horizontal loom. The equipment for weaving tapestries is so simple to use, it allows the artist a great amount of creative freedom.

Joseph Henry Sharp (jō´ zəf hen´ rē shärp)
(1859 – 1953)

About the Artist

Sharp was born in Ohio. He studied art in Germany, France, Belgium, and Spain. He wanted to develop an American form of art. In 1898, Sharp and two other art students began a wagon trip through the American West. They planned to sketch the areas they passed through. However, their wagon broke down near Taos in northern New Mexico. They saw that the area offered great subjects for their art. It had beautiful landscapes and an unusual blend of cultures.

In 1912, Sharp and his wife moved to Taos. By 1915, Sharp and five other artists had formed the Taos Society of Artists. Their work was successful, and soon a major art colony developed in Taos. Sharp painted the daily lives of different groups of Native Americans. He wanted to capture their lives before they were changed forever by contact with other cultures. President Roosevelt saw and admired Sharp's work. The President had the federal government supply Sharp with a place to live and work.

ABOUT ART HISTORY
Sharp is known as the father of the Taos art colony. He closely studied the lives of the Native Americans he painted. He wanted to understand them and make his paintings accurate. His written comments about his pictures are a valuable source of historical information.

ABOUT THE ARTWORK
Sharp painted individual and group portraits. Some of his subjects took part in major historic events, such as the Battles of the Little Big Horn and Wounded Knee. Sharp also painted still lifes of his own garden in Taos.

Buffalo Bill Historical Center, Cody, WY

ABOUT THE MEDIA
Sharp worked in oil paint.

ABOUT THE TECHNIQUE
At first, Sharp traveled and painted in a shepherd's wagon that had skylights and side lights. He painted by sunlight, moonlight, and lantern. He used color and light in his paintings to draw attention to detail, such as the look on a person's face.

Yves Tanguy (ēv tän gē′)
(1900 – 1955)

About the Artist

Tanguy was born in France. He became a merchant marine, sailing from port to port. At the age of 23, he happened to see a painting by the artist Chirico in the window of a French art gallery. Tanguy realized that the picture showed another world, different from the real world. Before that time, Tanguy had never thought of painting or even held a paintbrush. But he started a new career as an artist. At first, he struggled and destroyed his work. But in time, he developed a style that allowed him to express his feelings and ideas.

In 1925, Tanguy joined a group of French surrealist painters. They were each trying to paint their own visions of the world. In 1939, Tanguy moved to the United States. He married Kay Sage, an American surrealist painter, and became a U.S. citizen. He and his wife lived on a farm in Connecticut, far from others. There, they could paint without being bothered.

ABOUT ART HISTORY

Tanguy added to the surrealist movement by developing a style sometimes called *fantastic realism.* His paintings were like photographs of dreams.

ABOUT THE ARTWORK

Tanguy's pictures look like views into the unknown. His subjects look as if they live under the sea or on another planet. His paintings show a vast, bare wasteland. There, simple life forms struggle to live. The stillness of his

Yves Tanguy. (French). Indefinite Divisibility. *1942. Oil on canvas. 40 × 35 inches. Albright Knox Art Gallery, Buffalo, New York. Room of Contemporary Art Fund, 1945 © 1998 Artists Rights Society (ARS) New York/ADAGP, Paris.*

landscapes is similar to the stillness that astronauts discovered when they landed on the moon.

ABOUT THE MEDIA

Tanguy drew and painted in oil on canvas.

ABOUT THE TECHNIQUE

Tanguy once said that his paintings "unfolded" as he worked on them. He did not plan them. Sometimes he painted pictures upside down. When they were finished, he turned them around.

Martha Walter (mär´ thə wôl´ tər)
(1875 – 1976)

About the Artist

Walter was born in Philadelphia. Her family encouraged her to become an artist. She studied at the Pennsylvania Academy of Fine Arts, where artist William Merritt Chase introduced her to Impressionism. She received a scholarship to study painting in Paris, but she dropped out of art school because she felt it restricted her ideas too much. She set up her own studio in France. She was joined by many other young American women artists who were studying art abroad. In 1905, Walter returned to the United States and established her own studios in New York City and Boston, Massachusetts. By 1912, she had become famous for her paintings of beach scenes. She was still painting after the age of 90. She traveled to either Europe or Africa at least once a year.

ABOUT ART HISTORY

Walter was an Impressionist. Impressionism first developed in France in the late 1800s and early 1900s. Impressionist painters focused on capturing impressions of a moment. They tried to show the effects of reflected light.

ABOUT THE ARTWORK

Most of Walter's early works are scenes of modern city life in France. Later in her career, she became famous for her beach scenes. She painted most of these scenes in Gloucester, Massachusetts. These colorful paintings are filled with

Courtesy David David Gallery, Philadelphia

images of women and children at the ocean side, often under parasols and beach umbrellas.

ABOUT THE MEDIA

Walter worked in oils on canvas.

ABOUT THE TECHNIQUE

Walter's paintings are slightly abstract because she never used many lines. She concentrated on bright, vivid colors. She used especially intense colors to highlight ocean waves and the sky. Her paintings are filled with light and often have an unusual perspective.

Wang Chao (wong chou)
(c. 1500 – 1550)

About the Artist

Wang Chao (also spelled *Zhao*) was born in Anhui province, China, during the Ming dynasty. Anhui was a wealthy region at that time. That wealth helped support professional artists like Wang, who learned to imitate Chinese master painters. Wang was a muscular man, skilled in the martial arts and eager for adventure. He was sometimes arrested for his activities. At least once, he avoided jail by entertaining the judge with his paintings and poems.

ABOUT ART HISTORY

During Wang's lifetime, China had little contact with the outside world. Without any influence from artists in other nations, Chinese painters tended to copy ancient Chinese artists. Their art often focused on the beauty of objects. The Zhe (also spelled *Che*) School of painting was the main source of new ideas in Chinese art. However, it had lost its financial support by the time Wang began painting. Wang was one of the last painters from the Zhe School. He continued with old styles and did not move in new directions.

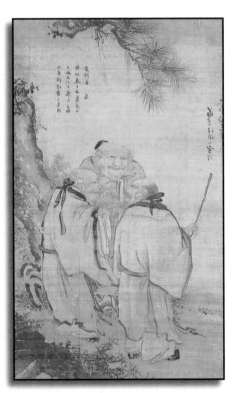

Wang Chao. (Chinese). The Three Stars of Happiness, Wealth, and Longevity. *c. 1500. Hanging scroll. Ink and light colors on silk. $62\frac{1}{2} \times 37\frac{1}{2}$ inches. Courtesy of the Kimbell Art Museum, Fort Worth, Texas.*

ABOUT THE ARTWORK

Wang painted landscapes and people. His images of birds and flowers, common subjects among Zhe School painters, were especially admired.

ABOUT THE MEDIA

This artist, like many Chinese painters, used mainly watercolors on paper. However, sometimes he experimented with other media, such as ink on silk.

ABOUT THE TECHNIQUE

Wang often bragged that he could paint pictures without making any sketches or drawings first.

Idelle Weber (i´ del web´ ər)
(1932 –   )

About the Artist

Weber was born in Chicago. She earned degrees in art at the University of California in Los Angeles. She began painting as a realist in the 1950s. She moved on to pop art in the 1960s. Now she is known as a photo-realist. She teaches art at the college level.

Courtesy Schmidt-Bingham Gallery.
Photo by Joe De Rosa

ABOUT ART HISTORY

Weber's style is so realistic that her paintings look like photographs. Photo-realists, also called super-realists, usually take photographs of their subjects. Then they paint from these photographs. They copy details with great accuracy. Weber and other photo-realists use slide projectors to project a photograph directly onto a canvas. Then they paint, using the photograph as a guide.

ABOUT THE ARTWORK

Weber usually paints still lifes. Her earlier paintings were mostly of fruits and vegetables. She switched to litter because she thinks it is more interesting. Her paintings look like snapshots of everyday items. For example, one painting shows a clutter of opened food cans, package wrappers, and other kitchen trash. She is more fascinated by containers than by what is in them. For this reason, empty crates and cartons often appear in her work. Weber does not paint trash because littering upsets her or because she cares about the environment. She just finds trash interesting!

ABOUT THE MEDIA

Weber creates oil paintings and prints.

ABOUT THE TECHNIQUE

Weber often finds her subjects on the streets of New York City. First, she chooses the best angle for her photograph. Sometimes she rearranges pieces of trash before snapping a picture. She often brings pieces of trash back to her studio to study before painting. She pays close attention to the color, shape, and texture of objects. She loves to show the velvet of a peach, for example, or the gleam of a package wrapper.

William T. Wiley (wil´ yəm wī´ lē)
(1937 –)

About the Artist

Wiley was born in Indiana but has lived mostly in California. He earned two degrees from the San Francisco Art Institute. He has taught at art schools and universities across the nation. He says that his students have taught him more than he has taught them. Wiley is married and has a son.

ABOUT ART HISTORY

In 1967, Wiley came to an important discovery. He realized that he could create art in any way he wanted. He did not have to worry about pleasing art critics. Wiley now has his own style. This style borrows from pop art by focusing on common objects. It also borrows from surrealism by placing these objects in unexpected settings. Wiley's style is a form of abstract art that combines common objects and personal symbols. Wiley was one of the first artists to include verbal humor in his art. He uses misspelled words and double meanings to help explain his outlook on life.

ABOUT THE ARTWORK

Wiley has explored the nature of art and the role of the artist. His work ranges from realistic landscapes to nearly abstract paintings. Some of his paintings look like children's games or strange maps. Perhaps

Jock McDonald

they are his way of showing another world or finding his way in this world. His recent paintings tend to be darker and moodier than his earlier ones. They give the sense that a terrible event is about to happen.

ABOUT THE MEDIA

Wiley creates oil paintings, watercolors, wash-and-ink drawings, murals, sculpture, and prints. Sometimes he adds feathers, string, sticks, or rope to his works.

ABOUT THE TECHNIQUE

Wiley sometimes places childish things in adult settings. For example, he might show a coloring or comic book in a landscape painting. He also makes real objects look unreal. Wiley often writes words, sentences, and even short poems over his paintings of images and symbols. For example, across one painting, he wrote, "These guise will try anything."

Double Saddlebag

About the Artist

The Sioux were native to the northern plains of North America, including land now known as Minnesota, the Dakotas, and Nebraska. They hunted their food and followed migrating herds of buffalo across the plains. During the mid-1800s, settlers and gold seekers killed many buffalo on the Sioux hunting grounds. By the late 1800s, the government was trying to force the Sioux onto reservations. Although groups led by Sitting Bull and Crazy Horse fought back, the Sioux eventually lost their freedom to choose where they lived. Now about half of the remaining Sioux live on reservations. The others live in cities across the United States, where many work to preserve Sioux traditions and crafts.

ABOUT THE ARTWORK

A double saddlebag was placed over a horse's back, behind the rider. The pockets on each side could hold the rider's food and other supplies. The Sioux used their highly decorated clothing and saddlebags only for ceremonies and other special occasions.

ABOUT THE MEDIA

Common materials for the Sioux saddlebags included buckskin (deer skin), canvas, porcupine quills or glass beads, sinew (thread made from animal tendons), and wool.

Artist unknown. Sioux. (United States). Double saddlebag. *1880. Buckskin, canvas, glass beads, straw, wood. $44\frac{3}{4} \times 13$ inches. Detroit Institute of Art, Detroit, Michigan.*

ABOUT THE TECHNIQUE

Long ago, Sioux women began making beads by cutting up dyed porcupine quills. (Some artists still use these kinds of beads.) Later, many of the women traded with the Europeans for glass beads. They sewed beads to their saddlebags and clothing in short rows to produce geometric designs. The symbolic meanings of these designs were not always the same for the maker and the wearer.

About the Artist

It is not known who built this particular mihrab. Mihrabs were built by skilled craftspeople. The structure was built by one group of workers, and the mosaic tiling was done by a separate group.

ABOUT ART HISTORY

Mihrabs are niches, or semicircular hollows, set into the middle of the qibla wall. The qibla wall is where people go to pray. The qibla wall is built outside a mosque, an Islamic communal house of prayer. The mihrab's purpose is to point the direction to Mecca. Mecca is the blessed city of the Islamic religion. Before mihrabs were built, a painted mark or a tree stump pointed the direction to Mecca. The first concave (hollowed out) mihrab was built in the Prophet's Mosque at Medina. Early mosques were built without mihrabs. Throughout history, mihrab decoration became more complicated, and mihrabs were decorated in the latest artistic styles. The most recent mosques, such as the one in the city of Bengal, have several mihrabs set in the qibla wall.

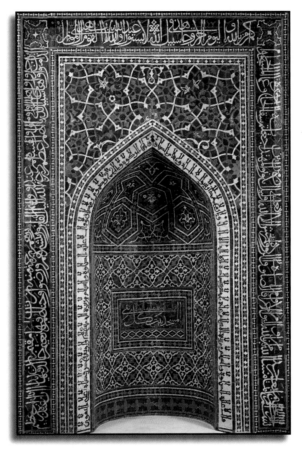

Mihrab. *Midrasa Imami, Isfahan (Iran). 1354. Glazed ceramic tiles. 11 feet 3 inches × 7 feet 6 inches. Metropolitan Museum of Art, New York, New York.*

ABOUT THE ARTWORK

This mihrab, unlike others, is from a school. Like other mihrabs, it has no figurative images. This means that there are no images of people, animals, or other living beings on the mihrab. Geometric and floral shapes are the most common images found on mihrabs.

ABOUT THE MEDIA

The mihrab's surface is made of glazed terra-cotta. Terra-cotta is a kind of clay.

ABOUT THE TECHNIQUE

The colors and designs on this mihrab were made with terra-cotta tiles in a process called *mosaic.* Each piece of terra-cotta was individually glazed with color. Then, the pieces were arranged to create the larger image that we see on the mihrab. Overall, mosaic is similar to doing a puzzle—small pieces join together to form a bigger picture.

Hat: Birds and Geometric Patterns

About the Artist

In the Andes Mountains of South America, in the region now known as Peru, the Inca empire slowly replaced an even older culture, the Wari. The ancient Inca empire had no coins or dollar bills. Handwoven cloth and clothing had so much value that it was often used in place of money. The Incas also had another use for clothing. Like the ancient Egyptians, they wanted to preserve the bodies of people who died. They often wrapped them in clothing and placed hats on their heads. Some ancient mummies have been found wrapped in dozens of layers of handwoven cloth.

ABOUT ART HISTORY

The Wari, and the Incas after them, decorated their clothing and other objects with animal images and geometric designs that represented ancient myths and wars. When the Spaniards invaded the Inca empire in the fifteenth century, they took advantage of the Incas' artistic skills. However, they wanted the Incas to use Spanish designs in their work. Some of the containers produced during this period have geometric patterns on one section and Spanish floral designs on another.

Artist unknown. (Peru). Hat: Birds and Geometric Patterns. *700–1000. Alpaca and cotton.* $4\frac{1}{2} \times 5$ *inches. The Seattle Art Museum, Gift of Jack Lenor Larson. Photo by Paul Macapia, Seattle, Washington.*

meanings, but these meanings have been lost over the centuries. The patterns, colors, and richness of the weaving indicated the status of the wearer.

ABOUT THE MEDIA

Andean craftspeople created clothing and hats from wool, cotton, or a combination of both.

ABOUT THE TECHNIQUE

The Incas wove designs into cloth but did not embroider it. In later periods, the Spanish introduced embroidery so that Incan artists could decorate garments for the Spanish Catholic Church. Today, Peruvian craftspeople sometimes use machine embroidery to add designs that ancient artists used to weave into garments.

ABOUT THE ARTWORK

The designs on ancient Wari and Inca hats and other clothing probably had religious

57

Covered Jar (Ming Dynasty)

About the Artist

This covered jar was probably made by a professional artist trained in the craft of pottery. There were many excellent potters in China during the Ming dynasty. They produced countless beautiful jars like this one.

ABOUT ART HISTORY

Covered Jar was made during the Ming dynasty. A dynasty is a series of rulers who come from the same family and rule a country for a long time. The Ming dynasty ruled China from 1368 to 1644. Many great works of art, such as porcelain and silk items, were produced during this time. These items were exported, or sent out of China, by boat to faraway places like Africa and Europe.

ABOUT THE ARTWORK

This Ming dynasty jar is painted with many designs and details. The designs around the base (bottom) and shoulder (rounded top below the lid) of the jar were used on many Ming jars. The underwater scene of catfish, seaweed, and floating leaves was another picture often found on jars from the Ming dynasty period. Porcelain jars like this one are very thin and delicate.

Artist unknown. (China). Covered Jar. 1522–1566. Porcelain painted with underglaze cobalt blue and overglaze enamels. 18½ inches high, 15¾ inches diameter. The Asia Society, New York, Mr. and Mrs. John D. Rockefeller 3rd Collection/Photo by Lynton Gardiner.

ABOUT THE MEDIA

This covered jar is made of porcelain. Porcelain is made by baking a fine white clay called *kaolin.* Paint was used to color the designs. Sometimes a clear gloss was painted over the entire surface to protect the jar and make it shine.

ABOUT THE TECHNIQUE

Jars like this one are made from lumps of soft, wet clay. The clay is put on a flat, spinning wheel and then shaped by the artist's hands as it spins. When the artist is happy with how it looks, the wheel is stopped and the jar is set out to dry.

Some of the designs on the jar were made by laying thin layers of clay over the jar's surface. Then, designs were cut into this thin layer. The jar was baked in a very hot oven to make it harden. The heat burned the designs into the jar in the places where the thin layer of clay was cut. The finished jar was painted with other colors like gold and green.

Sleeveless Shirt (two cats)

About the Artist

It is not known who crafted this sleeveless shirt. Most likely, it was made by a skilled weaver who worked during the time of the Incas, before the Spanish arrived in the mid-1500s.

Artist unknown. Coastal Inca (Peru). Sleeveless Shirt (two cats). *c. 1438–1532. Wool and cotton. Metropolitan Museum of Art, Nelson Rockefeller Collection, New York, New York.*

ABOUT ART HISTORY

No written history survives to tell us about Incan textile weaving. Archaeologists and art historians can only put together the pieces that they find. Luckily, Incan textiles were often buried in tombs and were not destroyed. Textile weaving was probably a main source of income in Inca civilization. Fabrics were also used as offerings to the Incan gods. Cloth has been found draped around gold statues. Textile patterns probably showed wealth and rank.

ABOUT THE ARTWORK

The two pumas facing each other in a mirror image is used often in Incan textile art. The puma cats are also standing directly across from each other. This is called symmetry. The animal figures are woven with different colored threads. Overall, Incan art uses images that are simple, noble, and restrained. This is different from earlier ancient Peruvian styles, which used more complicated geometric images arranged in patterns.

ABOUT THE MEDIA

The sleeveless shirt is woven with cotton. Other fabrics were woven using alpaca and llama wool, and even feathers.

ABOUT THE TECHNIQUE

Incan textiles were hand woven by skilled artisans. The designs on the fabrics were made in a number of different ways. They were painted on, stamped with a pattern, embroidered, and appliquéd.

About the Artist

Bakula Stanistawa of Poland created *Tree of Life*, but little beyond that is known about him. People learned from family members and school teachers how to make paper cuts. Paper cutting is a simple craft to learn.

ABOUT ART HISTORY

Paper cutting is a tradition in Germany, China, and Japan as well as in Poland. Polish paper cutting is called *wycinanki* (vee-chee-non-kee). This word comes from the verb *wynikac* (to cut). Paper cutting in Poland probably started in the rural farm areas sometime in the mid-nineteenth century. Social and economic factors may have allowed the peasants to use their time and resources to develop a unique paper-cutting art form. Paper cuts were used to decorate houses, furniture, and walls with bright colors. Often, paper cuts were made around Christmas and Easter. Polish paper cutting was most popular at the end of the nineteenth century and the beginning of the twentieth century.

ABOUT THE ARTWORK

This *Tree of Life* paper cut is a traditional

Artist unknown. (Poland). Tree of Life. *1962. Cut paper. International Folk Art Museum.*

Polish design. It looks like a silhouette because it is all black. However, many paper cuts used brilliant colors as well as black. This contrast of colors produced a surprising and vivid design. The *Tree of Life* is in the *kurpie* style. This means that it is a symmetrical design (the same on both sides) cut from a single piece of paper folded one time and then cut with motifs of spruce trees and angels. A one-color, symmetrical paper cut is called a *leluja* (leh-loo-yah).

ABOUT THE MEDIA

The *Tree of Life* is made from paper.

ABOUT THE TECHNIQUE

Wycinanki designs are made by folding a piece of paper, designing the image, and cutting the paper using scissors and sharp knives.

About the Artist

This work was made by an unknown artist and it is called Folk Art. This kind of art is made by self-taught artists. Folk artists usually think of their work as a hobby rather than a profession, and do it in their spare time.

ABOUT ART HISTORY

Washington's Headquarters was made sometime after 1876. Even though the work has no date, we know this because many of the images in the work have been cut out of Currier and Ives prints that were made after that date.

Currier and Ives was a firm of American lithographers, founded by Nathan Currier in 1834. Currier and Ives used a new printmaking process called *lithography* that had been invented in France. They printed black-and-white images, and then they hired women to hand color the prints with watercolor. Many artists became famous because Currier and Ives made their work popular.

ABOUT THE ARTWORK

It is assumed that this work was inspired by the 100th birthday of America. The cutouts from various Currier and Ives prints have been assembled to create the narrative parts of this image. The main image of George Washington on his horse is from the print *Washington, Crossing the Delaware: on the*

Artist unknown. (American). Washington's Headquarters 1780. At Newburgh, on the Hudson. Mixed-media. $21\frac{1}{4} \times 28$ inches. National Museum of American Art. Washington, DC, Art Resource, NY.

Evening of December 25th, 1776, Previous to the Battle of Trenton published in 1876. The men walking downhill with a cannon are also found in that print, but the line of soldiers receding into the background is taken from *Washington Taking Command of the American Army*, also printed in 1876. The printed title at the bottom of the collage is that of an undated Currier and Ives print.

ABOUT THE MEDIA

This collage is made from paper, straw, painted canvas, thread, mica, and metal. Notice the way the artist has applied the straw to represent walls, hillsides, and the water.

ABOUT THE TECHNIQUE

This artist created *Washington's Headquarters* in the same way that you would arrange and glue down found materials to make a collage.

Winged Genie

About the Artist

The ancient land of Assyria, or Assur, was located in northern Mesopotamia, which is now Iraq. Beginning in the eighth century B.C., during the reign of Ashur-nasir-pal II, Assyrian kings decorated their palace walls with huge carved scenes called reliefs. Some of these reliefs are now on display in the Brooklyn Museum in New York, the Louvre in Paris, and the British Museum in London.

ABOUT ART HISTORY

Assyrian artifacts from the ninth to the seventh centuries B.C. strongly influenced the art world during the late nineteenth and early twentieth centuries. Casts, or molds, were made of Assyrian reliefs for stage sets and costumes. Some French artists began to sculpt lions and tigers like those they saw in the reliefs. A dying lioness, portrayed in the Assyrian style, became the symbol of the German victory in Mesopotamia during World War I. Details from the reliefs were often used in biblical illustrations. The architecture shown in some reliefs became part of the American art deco style.

Artist unknown. (Assyria). Winged Genie.
c. 883–859 B.C. Alabaster. 91 inches high.
Brooklyn Museum of Art, New York, New York.

enemies, hunting lions, governing his people, overseeing crops, taking part in religious rituals, or simply relaxing in his garden. The Winged Genie, for example, depicts a supernatural being that supposedly helped the king during religious ceremonies. This and other panels were very detailed. In many cases, a long inscription across the center of each panel explained what was taking place.

ABOUT THE ARTWORK

The reliefs carved into palace walls were as tall as 90 inches. They often showed the king performing official duties such as fighting

ABOUT THE MEDIA

This type of relief was carved into a fine-textured stone called *alabaster.*

ABOUT THE TECHNIQUE

The reliefs were carved with hammers and chisels. Perhaps the craftsmen drew sketches before they began and had them approved by the king.

Necklace

About the Artist

This necklace was made by an unknown Berber artist in the Rif region of Morocco. The Berbers of North Africa live in the rugged Atlas, Rif, and Kabylia mountains and in the arid lands at the edge of the Sahara desert. Berber silversmiths are primarily male and Jewish.

ABOUT ART HISTORY

Berbers create art that is more Islamic than African in nature. As late as the fifteenth century, Jewish gold- and silversmiths fleeing the Spanish Inquisition settled in Northern Africa and introduced the jewelry-making techniques still used in the region.

Perhaps as a reaction to their difficult living environments in the mountains and desert, the Berber women wear enormous amounts of colorful beads. Beads bring color into a boring life. They also provide the spiritual protection associated with coral and amber, and the Koran, Islam's holy book. For Berber men, beads are a form of currency. A bead's worth is based on its weight, especially if it is made of silver. Silversmiths often melt down beads and rework them because the Berber prefer new beads to those worn by someone else.

ABOUT THE ARTWORK

This necklace was part of a ceremonial dowry piece. It features coral beads and silver coins on silver wire. Five silver Koranic boxes have

Artist unknown. (Morocco). Necklace. *Twentieth century. Beads and silver alloy. 14 inches long.*

been worked into the piece. The boxes are hollow and decorated with more silver. By including five of these boxes on the necklace, the artist has made a powerful statement. The number five is a magic number to the Moroccans. It symbolizes the khamsa, which is believed to ward off evil forces.

Muslims consider mathematics an integral part of art and believe that geometric ideas are the basis of all natural happenings.

ABOUT THE TECHNIQUE

The coral beads on the necklace are strung onto three strands of silver wire. The Koranic boxes are interspersed geometrically throughout the piece. Each silver coin is attached to its own silver wire and then is connected to the bottom strand of the necklace.

A Koranic box is made by heating the silver, then flattening it with a hammer before cutting it to the desired size. Then it is secured to a slab of wood. Then, it can be inlaid with enamel or decorated with stones.

Jar (Northern Song Period)

About the Artist

The artist who made this jar is unknown. The artist probably worked in one of the large ceramics factories located in Tz'u-hsien. Tz'u-hsien is in the province of Hopei in northeastern China.

ABOUT ART HISTORY

This jar was made during the Northern Song dynasty. The Northern Song dynasty lasted from A.D. 960 until A.D. 1279. There were many different types of pottery made during the Northern Song dynasty. This jar is of the Tz'u-chou type, named after the factory where it was made.

ABOUT THE ARTWORK

The Tz'u-hsien ceramics factory was famous for the special black-and-white decorative style seen on this jar. The technique used to create this ornate style is called *sgraffito*. This jar was probably a decorative object in a home or palace.

ABOUT THE MEDIA

This jar is made of porcelain. It is painted with white and black slip. Slip is a form of clay that is watered down and used as a coating.

Artist unknown. (China). Jar. *Northern Song Period, twelfth century. Stoneware with sgraffito design in slip under glaze. 12½ inches. The Asian Society, New York. Mr. and Mrs. John D. Rockefeller 3rd Collection/Photo by Lynton Gardiner.*

ABOUT THE TECHNIQUE

This jar was made using a potter's wheel. The potter placed a lump of porcelain clay onto the flat, spinning disc, then pulled the clay into the shape of a jar. The jar was then removed from the wheel and dried. When it was dry, it was decorated using the sgraffiato technique. The first step was to cover the jar with white slip. When the white slip dried, black slip was painted on in ornamental designs. Then, the artist carved details into the black slip with a thin knife. Lastly, the jar was baked in a very hot oven called a kiln.

Yam Mask

About the Artist

This mask was produced by a member of the Abelam society's Yam cult, located in Papua New Guinea. Art from this area is most often identified with religious beliefs. Because the religion is centered around males, the artists are almost always male. Some undecorated pots and weavings are made by women.

ABOUT ART HISTORY

The Yam cult's importance in Abelam society is especially evident at harvest time. During this season, the largest yams are decorated to show their owner's power. Because owners are associated with their yams in this way, they do not eat them. Instead, they trade them among other members of the clan.

Abelam society is characterized by many initiation ceremonies for males. One ceremony includes the making of basketry masks and carving and decorating the fronts of ceremonial houses. A mask may be worn by a man or used to decorate one of the largest yams from a harvest during a variety of ceremonies. Because the mask needs to be flexible to fit both, the Abelam make their masks out of basketry instead of wood.

ABOUT THE ARTWORK

During one ceremony in which young men are shown the mysteries of the spirit world, they wear masks like this and cover the rest of their bodies with shredded leaves.

Artist unknown. Abelam (Papua New Guinea). Yam Mask. Twentieth century. Yam fibers. $18\frac{3}{4} \times 13\frac{3}{8}$ inches. Nelson Atkins Museum of Art, Kansas City, Missouri. Gift of May Department Stores Co.

Any time the mask was used for an initiation ceremony or harvest festival, it was freshly painted and decorated.

Often, masks from New Guinea are fashioned after birds, fish, and other animals. In Abelam society, spirits are associated with pigs. However, the only reference to pigs seen here is in the shape of the ears.

ABOUT THE MEDIA

The artist used a mixture of natural materials found in New Guinea—wicker, pigments, natural fibers, feathers, and boar tusks—to make this mask.

ABOUT THE TECHNIQUE

The mask was made from wicker covered with standard paint colors found in New Guinea. Red pigment is made from ocher, while white pigment is taken from burned lime. Charcoal provided the black paint seen here. Artists usually mix their pigments with water, but sometimes they also use vegetable oils and tree-sap glazes.

Totem Pole

About the Artist

Totem poles are a traditional art form in Pacific Northwest native tribal culture. The Kwakiutl and the Haida cultures are two groups that made totem poles. They lived in what is now the Canadian province of British Columbia. Western culture changed the native cultures by introducing Western beliefs, tools, ideas, and ways of life. The introduction of Christian beliefs greatly affected the mythology and belief systems of the Kwakiutl and Haida cultures.

ABOUT ART HISTORY

Many Pacific Northwest people built totem poles. The Haida are considered the culture with the most developed wood-carving skills and artistic styles. As Western culture took root in the Pacific Northwest, the art of totem-pole carving was almost lost. It took a great deal of effort by master carvers and the American and Canadian governments to keep the art from dying. Totem poles are, thankfully, still being carved. Many of the newer poles tell mythological stories of people, spirits, and animals.

Artist unknown. Symmetrical View of a Totem Pole. *Photo. © Matthew McVay/Tony Stone Images, Inc. Stanley Park. Vancouver-B.C., Canada.*

ABOUT THE ARTWORK

This particular totem pole stands in Stanley Park in Vancouver, British Columbia. It has animals on it that represent traditional beliefs. The killer whale (the lord of the sea) and the wolf (the lord of the land) are linked by the frog. The Raven, who is considered the Creator God, is on top. The raven is also thought of as the source of light. These animals are half human, half god.

ABOUT THE MEDIA

Totem poles are carved from redwood cedar trees, then painted and stained.

ABOUT THE TECHNIQUE

A totem pole is usually carved by a team that includes a master carver and apprentices. Once a cedar tree is cut down (often the carver thanks the tree for giving up its life), the log is hollowed so that it dries evenly without splitting. Carvers shape the log by cutting away the outer sap wood. The master carver draws the figures onto the tree. Carving is done with a mallet and chisel. Finally, the totem pole is stained and painted. After the totem is finished, the people of the community eat a huge meal to celebrate.

About the Artist

The Egyptian artist of this painting remains unknown. *Portrait of a Boy* is an example of Fayum portraits, named for the area where most of these paintings have been found. Although the portrait resembles paintings of the Roman tradition, the funerary purpose and iconography reflect the Egyptian culture.

ABOUT ART HISTORY

In 30 B.C., the Romans took control of Egypt. For a while, they continued the Egyptian tradition of burying the dead in mummy cases. During this period, the stylized Egyptian drawings became more realistic and lifelike because of the Greek and Roman influences. By the fourth century A.D., bodies were buried in graves, without mummy cases or portraits. After the Arab invasion in the seventh century A.D., Egypt became a mostly Muslim nation, as it is today.

Artist unknown. (Egyptian). Portrait of a Boy. *Second Century A.D. 38 × 19 cm. Encaustic on wood. The Metropolitan Museum of Art, New York. Gift of Edward S. Harknes, 1918.*

ABOUT THE ARTWORK

Roman portraits differed greatly from the flat, stiff drawings of the ancient Egyptians. The use of highlights and shading gave depth and personality to the portraits. The faces were often shown at a slight angle, instead of in profile or with the eyes staring directly and blankly at the viewer.

ABOUT THE MEDIA

This work was painted with encaustic paint. This kind of paint had colors that were suspended in a wax medium. The wax was heated to a semiliquid state and then applied to the surface.

ABOUT THE TECHNIQUE

The artist may paint on any ground or surface. The paints were made by mixing dry pigments with molten white, refined beeswax plus a small amount of resin from a warm palette. The manipulation of the paint by brush or palette knife was assisted by warming and chilling the surface. A final heat treatment was done by passing a heat source over the surface. This fused the painting and bonded it into its permanent form without altering it. A gentle polishing with soft cotton brought out a dull, satiny sheen. When cool, the picture was finished.

Bayeux Tapestry

About the Artist

The artist who drew and embroidered the huge Bayeux Tapestry is unknown. Art historians think the tapestry was made in England in the early Middle Ages. They believe it was designed by an illustrator and then finished by embroiderers.

ABOUT ART HISTORY

The Bayeux Tapestry is a unique piece of art. Wall paintings that recorded historical events were common. Tapestries that did so were not. The Bayeux Tapestry tells the story of the Battle of Hastings and William the Conqueror. The tapestry was severely damaged from constant rolling and unrolling. From 1812 to 1814, it was restored by Charles Stothard, a British artist. The tapestry now hangs in the Centre Guillame le Conquerant (The Center of William the Conqueror) in Bayeux, France.

ABOUT THE ARTWORK

The Bayeux Tapestry is a long and narrow strip of linen with figures embroidered on it. The story of William the Conqueror and the Battle of Hastings takes up about half of the

Artist unknown. Bayeux Tapestry. Detail of Norman Cavalry Charging in the Battle of Hastings. *1070–1080. Embroidered wool on linen. 20 inches high × 231 feet. Musée de Peinture, Bayeux, France.*

tapestry. Halley's Comet is shown in a panel called "These Men Marvel At the Star." The border of the tapestry is decorated with fantastic birds and beasts. The border also tells some of Aesop's fables, including "The Fox and the Crow" and "The Wolf and the Lamb."

ABOUT THE MEDIA

The Bayeux Tapestry is made of linen, and is embroidered with wool and colored thread.

ABOUT THE TECHNIQUE

It is unknown exactly how the Bayeux Tapestry was created. Art historians think that an illustrator designed the images on the tapestry. Then, embroiderers filled in the drawings with the wool and colored thread.

About the Artist

An individual of the Karajas, a native Amazonian people living in Brazil, made this headdress. Five hundred different native cultures live in the Amazon. Each culture has its own language, beliefs, and customs. All believe that they share the forest with the animals and the plants. When Europeans first arrived in South America, as many as 12 to 15 million native people lived in the Amazon. Since then, millions of native Amazons have died from Western diseases or cruel treatment. Native Amazons are still struggling to keep their lands and culture.

ABOUT ART HISTORY

Creating objects for rituals is an native Amazonian tradition. Objects created for ritual use, like this Karaja headdress, show the culture's belief that animals share their powers with humankind.

ABOUT THE ARTWORK

This feather headdress looks like a big red and orange sunburst. The part worn closest to the head is made of woven reeds and leaves. Scarlet and red-and-green macaw feathers burst out of this tightly woven area. The orange feathers form a circle close to the wearer's face. The red-and-green feathers branch out towards the sky. Feathered headdresses are worn by older men and

Artist unknown. (Brazil). Feather Headdress. *Early twentieth century. Feather headdress mounted on split reeds. Courtesy of the Smithsonian National Museum of the American Indian, NY. Collected by Frances-Gow-Smith. Photo by David Heald.*

political leaders in the Karaja culture. These headdresses are a symbol of bravery and authority. Usually a headdress is worn only during celebrations and other special occasions.

ABOUT THE MEDIA

This headdress is made from reeds, palm leaf spines, cotton cord, and scarlet and red-and-green macaw feathers. The artist may have used a needle made of plant material.

ABOUT THE TECHNIQUE

The Karaja artist who made this headdress wove together reeds and palm leaf spines with cotton cord to form the base of the crown. Then, feathers were sewn to the base.

About the Artist

It is not known who made this shirt section. Textile weaving was an important part of ancient Peruvian culture, and Peruvians were outstanding weavers. This shirt section was probably made by a skilled weaver.

ABOUT ART HISTORY

The designs on this shirt section are from the Tiahuanaco culture, also known as Middle Horizon. The images on the fabric were important because they illustrated Tiahuanaco ideas. When people wore this kind of shirt or other clothing (such as ponchos) showing similar designs, they spread their ideas wherever they went. These images were probably copied from the Gateway of the Sun at Tiahuanaco. The Gateway of the Sun was an ancient center of worship.

Artist unknown. *Coastal Huari (Peru).* Shirt Section. *c. A.D. 600–1000. Alpaca wool and cotton. 21 × 12$\frac{7}{8}$ inches. The Metropolitan Museum of Art, The Michael C. Rockefeller Memorial Collection, bequest of Nelson A. Rockefeller, 1979, New York, New York.*

ABOUT THE ARTWORK

The patterns on the shirt section are geometric, they have many angles and very few curves. For example, images of faces are flat, not shadowed to look three dimensional. Some people think this is because the ancient Peruvians did not want to offend the gods by representing them realistically.

ABOUT THE MEDIA

The shirt section is made of alpaca and llama wool.

ABOUT THE TECHNIQUE

The shirt section was hand woven by skilled weavers.

Thunderbird Shield

About the Artist

The Absaroke were one of the Plains cultures. They spoke the Siouan language and were called Crow. They lived mostly around the Yellowstone River and its territories and were a hunting culture. They were enemies of the Sioux. In battle, a warrior wanted to bring as much supernatural help, or medicine, as possible with him. This protection was in the warrior's shield, facial paint, and decorations on his garments. The shield, however, was the only form of mystical help that also provided physical defense against enemy weapons.

ABOUT ART HISTORY

To obtain medicine, young men of the Plains cultures would go on a Vision Quest. For four days, a boy went off by himself and fasted. During or after this fast, he might have a vision or dream. Usually such a vision included an animal giving the boy a special power and specific rituals to make his power effective. Part of the ritual would include a shield design.

ABOUT THE ARTWORK

The owner of this shield received his personal medicine from the thunderbird. The symbols representing the thunderbird were painted onto the buffalo hide, which was then covered with feathers. The ends of some of the feathers were cut on a slant. Plains peoples cut feathers to signify cutting an enemy's throat.

Artist unknown. Absaroke (United States). Thunderbird Shield. *c. 1830. Buffalo hide shield with inner cover decorated with paintings and feathers. Courtesy of the Smithsonian National Museum of the American Indian, NY. Collected by W. Wildschut. Photo by David Heald.*

ABOUT THE MEDIA

The thunderbird shield is made from buffalo hide, paint, and feathers.

ABOUT THE TECHNIQUE

The shield was made from stretched buffalo hide. The black, yellow, and red paints were made from powdered earth substances mixed with a glutinous substance obtained from boiling hide scrapings. The color of paint used was not common. It looks bluish-green in the upper left. It was probably obtained through trade. The artist attached feathers to the buffalo hide.

About the Artist

Skilled artisans practiced the art of rug weaving before, during, and after the Ottoman empire. City registers list rug makers as specific professional craftspeople.

ABOUT ART HISTORY

There is not much remaining history about the art of rug weaving. Bursa, the former Ottoman capital was a highly renowned silk-weaving city, and a possible manufacturing center of Turkish Ottoman rugs. These rugs make up only about one percent of all Turkish rug designs. In fact, a floor covering like the one pictured was made only in the second half of the sixteenth century and in the seventeenth century. The Ottoman patterns greatly influenced later Anatolian weavers. They changed curvilinear patterns to more angular ones. These floor coverings are also known as Ottoman court rugs because they were designed specifically for the Ottoman court.

Artist unknown. (Turkey). Early sixteenth century. Floor Covering *(Detail). 490.2 × 268 cm. Velvet. Photograph © 1996 Detroit Institute of Arts, Gift of Edsel B. Ford, Detroit, Michigan.*

ABOUT THE ARTWORK

This Ottoman floor covering is woven in a design that closely reflects the designs that were so much a part of the Ottoman courts. These patterns were not woven until at least 1550. A main feature of the rugs is their graceful leaves and blossoms, lancet leaves, and palmette blossoms.

ABOUT THE MEDIA

The Ottoman floor covering was made of dyed wool thread.

ABOUT THE TECHNIQUE

The detailed design of Ottoman rugs is determined by the knot of the thread used. The more knots, the finer the pattern. The Turkish Ottoman floor covering was woven by master rug weavers and their skilled workers.

About the Artist

The Teton Lakota culture is a branch of the Sioux. Over the years, the Teton Sioux's differences in speech patterns divided the group into three peoples—the Lakota, Nakota, and Dakota Sioux. Sioux were Plains people who lived in the area surrounding the upper Mississippi River. They were known for their warriors. Through the nineteenth century, the Sioux fought hard against white westward expansion.

ABOUT ART HISTORY

There were many changes in Plains beadwork after the 1880s. By this time, women had more time to develop both beadwork and quillwork as an art form. Floral patterns were probably introduced to them through formal European-style education or intermarriage. The Teton Lakota produced art with curving and twisting lines before contact with non-natives, so they easily adapted the stylized floral patterns to their art.

ABOUT THE ARTWORK

Parasols were not commonly made by Plains women, because they were not considered necessities. Perhaps the artist who constructed this parasol thought of it as a status symbol. The two floral patterns alternate on the six panels of the parasol.

Artist unknown. Teton Lakota. (United States).
Parasol. *Buckskin, quilled and beaded. $25\frac{1}{4} \times 23$ inches. Courtesy of the Smithsonian National Museum of the American Indian, NY. George H. Bingenheimer Collection. Photo by David Heald.*

Great care was paid to the detail in the embroidery and beadwork.

ABOUT THE MEDIA

The fabric of the parasol is deerskin. The artist embroidered floral patterns with porcupine quills and beadwork.

ABOUT THE TECHNIQUE

The artist used two methods of decorating this parasol. Embroidery with porcupine quills was a common decoration added to clothing and other objects in the early 1800s. Embroiderers would soak quills in water to soften them, then dye them with vegetable coloring. The beads used here are tiny "seed beads" that were popular after the middle of the nineteenth century.

Jar (Middle Jomon period)

About the Artist

This artist is unknown. The jar was made during the Middle Jomon period of Japanese history. During this period, daily life consisted of hunting, gathering roots and berries, fishing, and collecting shellfish. The Jomon created a great number of ceramics in a wide variety of styles.

ABOUT ART HISTORY

The earliest Jomon pottery was created before 10,000 B.C. It is the oldest known pottery in the world. Ancient ceramics show how society changes over the centuries. Archaeologists study the shape, texture, methods of manufacture, and location of pottery to learn about changes in food preparation, ceremonies, politics, and religious beliefs of a society. During the Middle Jomon period (about 2500 to 1500 B.C.) new forms of ceramics, such as hanging lamps and pots with raised feet, were created. Some new shapes included shells and fish.

ABOUT THE ARTWORK

These ceramics are textured with cord and look a little like baskets because of their surface designs. The effects of the Jomon texturing process are stunning. Many pieces of this period feature overhanging rims or flared rims with pieces that stick out. Another common feature of this period is the use of

Artist unknown. (Japan). Middle Jomon period. Jar. c. 3000–2000 B.C. Earthenware clay with applied, incised, and cord-marked decoration. 27½ inches. The Metropolitan Museum of Art, New York, New York. The Harry G. C. Packard Collection of Asian Art, Gift of Harry G. C. Packard and Purchase, Fletcher, Rogers, Harris Brisbane, Dick and Louis V. Bell Funds, Joseph Pulitzer. Bequest and the Annenberg Fund, Inc. Gift 1975.

raised bands to define the shoulder area of a piece. Middle Jomon ceramics may have been used for preparing, serving, eating, drinking, and storing food and drink.

ABOUT THE MEDIA

These ceramics were created out of clay and decorated with cords and sticks. Open fire, not a kiln, was used to fire the ceramics.

ABOUT THE TECHNIQUE

Middle Jomon ceramics were hand built with clay coils. The surfaces were decorated when the clay was as hard as leather. These decorations were made with twisted cords or cord-wrapped sticks, which were pressed into the clay. Sometimes cords were intertwined and rolled over the surface to create an interesting texture. Multiple cords, twisted in different "directions or knotted, made a great variety of decorations. After decoration, the pots were fired in open bonfires.

Child's Beaded Shirt

About the Artist

Native Plains women usually made clothing for members of their family. Their designs were usually abstract and geometric. Most often, the patterns in these designs were balanced. This shirt was probably made by an individual of the Cheyenne or Teton Dakota cultures.

ABOUT ART HISTORY

Before contact with non-natives, Plains people decorated most clothing with paint and porcupine quill embroidery. Native peoples were fascinated with the beads they discovered through trade. The earliest beads were large. They were called pony beads because traders brought them west in pony pack trains. By the 1850s, Plains people also had access to smaller beads called *seed beads.* After the Civil War, many styles of beadwork developed. The golden age of Native American beadwork began in the 1880s. By this time, women had more time to devote to beadwork as an art form and more colors of beads to use. The women also added European designs and patterns to their handiwork.

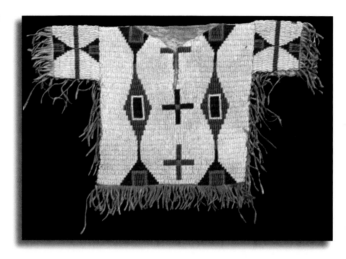

Artist unknown. Northern Cheyenne or Teton Dakota (United States). Child's Beaded Shirt. *c. 1865. Buffalo hide, glass seed beads. 33.5 × 58.5 cm. Courtesy of the Dallas Museum of Art, Textile Purchase Fund.*

ABOUT THE ARTWORK

The artist used red, white, and blue beads in this child's shirt. The designs on the shirt were common in the Central Plains area. Balance was created by repeating shapes and lines in the same colors down each side and on the sleeves of the shirt.

ABOUT THE TECHNIQUE

Two basic techniques were used to stitch beads to skins. The first stitch was known as the spot or overlay stitch. Artists threaded beads on a sinew. With a second sinew, they sewed the beaded sinew onto the skin by stitching between every second or third bead. The second stitch was called the *lazy stitch.* Beads were threaded onto a sinew, and only the ends of the sinew were attached to the skin. The first method produces a smooth surface; the second method produces a rougher surface.

Ishtar Gate

About the Artist

Many skilled workers built the Ishtar Gate. It was planned under the rule of Nebuchadezzar II in the sixth century B.C. in the ancient city of Babylon.

ABOUT ART HISTORY

The Hanging Gardens of Babylon were one of the Seven Wonders of the World. These Gardens, along with the Ishtar Gate and other structures, were all a part of Nebuchadnezzar's rebuilding of Babylon. The Babylonian civilization ended around 331 B.C. In 1899, German archaeologists began to excavate the ancient ruins. They rebuilt the Ishtar Gate (a process that took many years) and it now stands on display in Berlin's Vorderasiatisches Museum.

Artist unknown. (Babylonia). Ishtar Gate. *c. 605–562 B.C. State Museum, Berlin, Germany. Erich Lessing/Art Resource, NY.*

ABOUT THE ARTWORK

Ishtar was the Babylonian goddess of love, fertility, and warfare. The gate named for her was made of baked and glazed brick, then decorated with a procession of bulls and Babylon's patron god, Marduk. The bull represented the weather god, Adad. Marduk was a remarkable, scaly dragon beast who had a horned serpent head, feline front legs, eagle talons on the back legs, and a tail with a scorpion stinger at the end. The foundations of the gateway reached 40 feet into the ground. Its double gateway was surrounded by four towers.

ABOUT THE MEDIA

The Ishtar Gate was made of brick, glaze, and paint.

ABOUT THE TECHNIQUE

Nebuchadnezzar wrote about the making of the Ishtar Gate in his Great Stone Slab Inscription:

"I laid their foundations at the water table with asphalt and bricks and had them made of bricks with blue stone. . . . I placed wild bulls and ferocious dragons in the gateways and thus adorned them with luxurious splendor so that mankind might gaze on them with wonder."

First Bishop of Ravenna Apse Mosaic

About the Artist

The artisans who created this work were unknown craftspeople.

Artist Unknown. (Italy). Ravenna Apse Mosaic *(Detail).* 549 A.D. The Church of Saint Apollinaris, Ravenna, Italy. Scala/Art Resource, New York.

ABOUT ART HISTORY

Mosaics have been used for centuries to decorate the walls and floors of many churches, mosques, and other buildings. Mosaics have been found in many countries in Europe, the Middle East, and North Africa. Mosaics in Europe often show religious themes and people from politics, the church, or the Bible. Mosaics in the Middle East and Africa are usually very decorative. They have complicated patterns and designs. Over the years, many of the most beautiful mosaics have been destroyed, but this one has survived in fairly good condition.

ABOUT THE ARTWORK

This mosaic is in the Church of Saint Apollinare, which is in the city of Classe, Italy. It was created between A.D. 533 and 549. This colorful design is on the inside wall of the altar end of the church. The sheep represent the twelve apostles. They stand on either side of Saint Appollinare.

ABOUT THE MEDIA

Mosaics are made with small cubes of colored enamel, glass, or marble. They are attached to the wall with mortar or cement.

ABOUT THE TECHNIQUE

The small cubes that make up the mosaic are called *tesserae.* These pieces reflect a lot of light so that the pictures look very colorful and bright. Different colored tesserae are placed very close together on a wall, like a puzzle, to make patterns or pictures. They are held to the wall with cement, plaster, or another material that will make them stick.

Duncan House Bedroom

About the Artist

Many hands went into creating the bedroom at Duncan House in Haverhill, Massachusetts. The Derby family in New England crafted most of the large canopy bed. John Doggett (a mirror frame maker), John Ritto Penniman (an ornamental painter), and Thomas Whitman all helped to fashion the bed, which was finished in the workshop of Thomas Seymour. Other craftspeople who made items in the Duncan House bedroom remain unknown. The design is from the Scottish cabinetmaker, Duncan Phyfe.

ABOUT ART HISTORY

The furniture in this bedroom is an example of the Federal style, which was most popular in the decades after the Revolutionary War. It was influenced by styles from England and France. Federal period rooms were tall and spacious, had high ceilings, and large windows that sometimes extended down to the floor. Furniture was placed symmetrically (meaning the same on both sides). It was delicate, ornate, and filled with straight lines and geometric shapes.

ABOUT THE ARTWORK

The tables at the end of the bed were popular during the Federal period. They were used as

Artist unknown. Duncan House Bedroom. *1805. Bed-sitting room. Haverhill, Massachusetts.*

sewing or worktables. This bedroom is ornate and detailed. The throw rug is a popular geometric design of the Federal period.

ABOUT THE MEDIA

The Duncan House bedroom is made of many materials. The bed is made of mahogany wood, paint, and gilding. Other materials include brass, plaster, and silk.

ABOUT THE TECHNIQUE

As you can see by the details on the furniture, everything made by these artisans was very intricate and required special tools. Making these pieces involved wood carving, carpentry, metalworking, weaving, and sewing.

Bedroom (cubiculum nocturnum)

About the Artist

Boscoreale is an area about one mile north of Pompeii. Long ago, wealthy Romans had large country villas in Boscoreale. Many villas in Boscoreale were buried by the eruption of Mt. Vesuvius in A.D. 79. A villa, excavated in the late 1900s, contained a treasure of ancient art that was preserved and is now exhibited in the Louvre and other museums.

ABOUT ART HISTORY
The villa was probably built during the first century B.C. The paintings saved from the villa are examples of the late Second Style, which grew out of an early Hellenistic painting style.

ABOUT THE ARTWORK
The bedroom from the villa at Boscoreale has been reassembled inside New York's Metropolitan Museum of Art. The walls were painted to look like views of the villa's grounds. They are divided into panels by Corinthian columns. Metal and glass objects seem to sit on shelves along the walls and cast shadows. On one wall there is a painting of an entrance that seems to lead to another, more fantastic villa. The elaborate door is inlaid with tortoise shell and has bronze lion heads as knockers. Another wall looks like the mouth of a cave. A small statue standing

Artist unknown. (Roman). Bedroom *(cubiculum nocturnum). 40–30 B.C. Fresco on lime plaster. 8 feet 8½ inches × 19 feet 1⅞ inches × 10 feet 11½ inches. The Metropolitan Museum of Art, New York, New York. Rogers Fund, 1903. Photograph by Shecter Lee.*

guard shows that someone lives in the cave. A window in the bedroom seems to look out over a garden and fountain. Other panels suggest scenery from plays. Whoever directed the painting enjoyed fantasy and wanted to impress visitors to the villa.

ABOUT THE MEDIA
Many of the wall paintings are frescoes, painted while the plaster on the wall was still "fresh" or wet.

ABOUT THE TECHNIQUE
Frescoes are made by first covering the walls with layers of plaster. After the plaster is dry, the artist does a rough sketch. Then, the artist applies another coat of plaster and paints on it while it is still wet. This technique produces a painting that becomes a permanent part of the wall.

Cover of Armenian Book

About the Artist

This cover was done in 1691 by Astuatsatur Shahamir, from the Armenian city of Kayseri, home of skilled silversmiths and goldsmiths. The inside illustrations were completed by artists from the city of Cilicia, who were known for their painting skill. The words in the book were written by a scribe named Gregor. He gilded some letters in the first part of the book.

ABOUT ART HISTORY

Christianity became the official religion of Armenia during the fourth century. At that time, the pagan art of Armenia began to disappear as a new kind of art took over. Armenian artists used scenes from the Gospel and images of Christianity to decorate their churches and to illustrate their manuscripts. Existing illustrated Armenian manuscripts date from the ninth to the seventeenth centuries. They are based on early Christian and Byzantine art, but they tend to be more lively and dramatic.

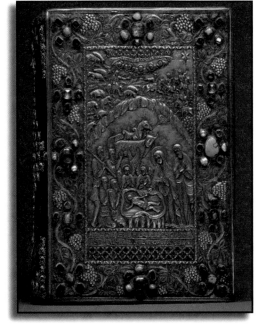

Artist unknown. (Armenia). Cover of Armenian Book. *Sixteenth century. Carved and hammered silver, gilded and enameled, and set with hammered silver, gilded and enameled, and set with jewels, rubricated. $10\frac{1}{4} \times 7\frac{3}{8}$ inches. The Metropolitan Museum of Art, New York, New York. Gift of Mrs. Edward S. Harkness, 1916.*

book cover contains floral, geometric, and animal patterns. The center panel shows the shepherds worshipping the Christ Child and the Magi following the star. The cover was engraved in silver. The grapevine in the design has a green enamel background and contains precious and semi-precious stones. The back cover shows Christ's resurrection, including a tomb with a sleeping guard and two standing soldiers. The spine of the cover is also decorated with semiprecious jewels.

ABOUT THE ARTWORK

Like other illustrations of this period, this

ABOUT THE MEDIA

This book cover was created from silver and semiprecious stones.